CRACKER INGENUITY

Tips from the Trailer Park for the Chronically Broke

CRACKER INGENUITY

P. T. ELLIOTT *and* **E. M. LOWRY**

ILLUSTRATIONS BY MIKE RUNDLE

St. Martin's Griffin
New York

www.stmartins.com

Book design by Michelle McMillian

Library of Congress Cataloging-in-Publication Data

Elliott, P. T.
  Cracker ingenuity: tips from the trailer park for the chronically broke/P. T. Elliott and E. M. Lowry.
      p. cm.
ISBN 0-312-29082-9
  1. Home economics—Humor. 2. Consumer education—Humor. I. Lowry, E. M. II. Title
TX295.E45 2003
640'.2'07—dc21
                                                          2002036893

First Edition: March 2003

10   9   8   7   6   5   4   3   2   1

NOTE TO READER

Due to the litigious society in which we live, we find it necessary to warn you in advance that many of the activities described herein are dangerous and some are illegal and might get you sent to heaven or prison or both. We don't recommend you do them. Nor do we recommend you stay home, lock your doors, and do nothing.

CONTENTS

ACKNOWLEDGMENTS

Thanks to our agent, Giles Anderson, and to our editor, Brad Wood, for getting this book off the ground. And thanks to Mike Rundle for his great illustrations. Thanks also to the folklorists, the Alexanderians, the Elliotts, the Lowrys, the Gildeas, Leo Kropywiansky, and to the many family members and friends who helped make this book happen.

Thanks to all those who contributed their inventions and insights, especially Butch Anthony, Mike Luster, and Mark Powers, without whose help this book wouldn't be nearly so full. Also thanks to Joe Arcidiacono, Brad Bowling, Demorge Brown, Mitch Butler, Bruce Campbell, Roby Cogswell, Russell Davenport, Norm Deveraux, Marshall Dostal, Kelly Farewell, Alexander Georges, Erika Hanson, Andrew Hill, Ethan Jackson, Simon Kahn, Colleen Kelley, Kevin Kennedy, the Keys, Ed Lanolin, Bob and Irene Leonard, Valerie Levitt, David Loeb, Roger Manley, Cindy McTamany, Isabelle Moore, Mark O'Connor, Trish Potenza, Erin Roth, Erica Rothschild, John Sammon, Hank Schleber, Renard Steiff, Jason Stevens, "Pop," Stuart M. Teigen, Jason Twite, Genevieve Watson, and Jessica Zweback.

INTRODUCTION

"Necessity is the mother of invention," they say, and it's the truth.

Cracker Ingenuity celebrates the great inventions of people who've been broke for a long time and will be broke for at least that long again. And while these inventions are often inspired by a lack of cash, they reveal the wealth of ideas out there for making do with what you have. This book proves that the "secret to living well" is knowing the difference between just getting by, and getting by in *style*.

Okay, so *Cracker Ingenuity* may not be about inventing computer chips or electricity, but who's to say that building picket fences from pallet boards and monster BBQs out of spent car parts isn't almost as important? The tools of cracker ingenuity are everyday objects like cans and carburetors, tires, wires, and pool chlorine. And in the all-American realms of trucks, trailers, and Vienna weenies, *Cracker Ingenuity* revels in the simple brilliance of lift kits and AstroTurf carpeting. Folklorists dress it up and call it "vernacular technology," and regular folks call it "jerry-rigging"—but really, this kind of genius is nothing less than the heart of a long American tradition of adaptation, invention, and survival. If nothing else, this book proves that the pioneer spirit lives on. Seriously, how can you consider yourself a self-sufficient, resourceful person if you don't know how to disable the governor on your drive-mower so it can go sixty miles an hour? This book has tips on how to *make things happen* with the crap that's been lying around the house since before you were born—and a lot of these ideas are even legal. That said, *Cracker Ingenuity* is dedicated to the small glories of living, broke.

House and Home

Living "in a pinch" is what this book is all about, and there is no better ally for getting by than your own backyard. This section is dedicated to cracker ingenuity around the home and how, with a little free time and enough raw material, you can build an empire. . . or a porch attachment.

TRAILERS

There is no better place to start talking about cracker genius in the house and home than the home that is not a house—the trailer.

Trailers have been around for almost a century. As early as 1915, people were transforming their cars into houses to ride the open road. The Tourist Camp Body Company of Chicago made the first commercially built trailer in 1921. Trailerites of this era were called "Tin Can Tourists," or "TCTs," because they drove tin cans, ate from tin cans, and left a mess of tin cans behind them. Tin cans aside, by the late twenties, trailers were considered an amazing invention on par with airships and submarines. They were called "modern prairie schooners" at the time, and they spread like brushfire.

Even Mickey Mouse had a trailer. Walt Disney's 1938 classic cartoon, "Mickey's Trailer," showed Mickey riding high in a trailer that underwent a series of ingenious transformations. A bump in the road turned the dining room table into a bathtub; the picket fence and lawn could be reeled in through the back door; and the blue blue sky

"A house-car of the 1920s was a marvel to its owners and admirers. Its compactness and completeness were highly regarded as virtues, examples of ingenuity."

—ROGER B. WHITE,
HOME ON THE ROAD

itself folded neatly up into the chimney—sun, clouds, and all.

Early mobile homes prided themselves on having foldout gadgets that would make yachtsmen turn a jealous green. Many came with foldout king-size beds, full kitchens, porches, and even a foldout cage for the pet that became the symbol of life on the road—the canary.

With all this ground-breaking invention, how did the trailer park get such a crappy reputation? How did trailers come to be associated with the snaggle-toothed, the perverted, and the chronically dispossessed? Like everything else, it boils down to some fact, some fiction, and some vicious PR.

Trailers took a turn from tourist marvel to basic survival when America's fortunes fell between the two world wars. The first permanent trailer parks appeared during the Depression, and people traveling west set up house-car camps all the way to California. In 1935, Roger Ward Babson, dean of the American Financial Advisors who predicted the market crash of 1929, made his second most famous prediction: "Within two decades one out of every two Americans will be living in a trailer." At this time, everyone was stone broke, and trailerites were seen as vagabonds: mooching off permanent communities, conning the local rubes, and skipping town when it was time to pay the bills. The Establishment was less than thrilled when people began to abandon costly public housing to hit the road. Resentment grew as police forces, schools, and hospitals found they couldn't cope with the roving population, and the notion of "trailer trash" was born. Trailerites gained reputations as criminals and carriers of vile diseases like smallpox and typhoid fever. Their reputation grew until, in the forties, FBI Director J. Edgar Hoover declared their mobile villages to be "camps of crime" and "dens of vice and corruption haunted by nomadic prostitutes, hardened criminals, white slavers, and promiscuous college students."

But it hasn't been all thievery and mayhem: In the fifties, a company called Airstream bolstered the trailer image when it came out with a famously good-looking aluminum "land yacht." Even Lucille Ball and Desi Arnez rode through the full trailer experience in the 1954 film *The Long Long Trailer*. The celebrity-chic of trailers continues today: In 1993, Sean Penn set up shop in a twenty-seven-foot Airstream trailer in Malibu when his house burned down. He decorated the trailer with guns and pictures of Hemingway and Charles Bukowski.

Some 20 million Americans currently live *full time* in an estimated 9 million mobile homes. And there are still mobile villages, like Slab City in Southern California, where trailerites gather for the winter to escape the harsh climates of their more permanent addresses.

THE TRAILER INGENUITY TEST (T.I.T.)

You're not trailer-true unless you're a full-timer, but not everyone has what it takes to live in a double-wide year round. Crafty full-timers have devised ways to deal with everything from claustrophobia to marital strife.... Do you have what it takes?

★ TAKE THE T.I.T. AND SEE IF YOU MEASURE UP ★

Two preliminary questions
How tall are you?
How much do you weigh?
If you're over six-two or two hundred fifty pounds, a word to the wise: Too big is too big. You won't fit. Trailer doors are usually only two feet wide or less (regular doors are two and a half feet), and ceilings aren't anywhere near the room standard, eight feet. And while smaller is better for trailer-sized purposes, beware. . . being too tiny can also cut your intimidation-factor advantage with the neighbors.

T.I.T. #1: Flying Solo

Trailer life: Can you hack it by yourself?

1. Your relationships with your landlords:
   A. Are generally pretty good. You've never been evicted or moved out of a place because of a personal disagreement with the landlord.
   B. Are fair. You've been late on a couple of checks. Got a complaint or two. Maybe an eviction notice, but everything worked out OK.
   C. Are not so good. You often get into serious fights with landlords, but you stay put, no matter what.
   D. Are not so good for you. You often get into serious fights with landlords and then move, breaking the windows on the way out because you know you'll never get your security deposit back.
   E. Are not so good for them. You fight and move out all the time, but you have an attack dog, so you always get your deposit back.
2. You stand in a room, and you can reach the ceiling easily with your hand. You:
   A. See it as a convenient place to put Post-it notes.
   B. See it as an opportunity for isometric exercises.

C. Feel trapped, cramped, boxed in . . . but ignore it.
D. Get out of the room as soon as possible.
E. Don't notice.
3. You find airplane seats to be:
   A. Cool because they recline at just the right angle to crush the laptop of the suit sitting behind you.
   B. Fine.
   C. Uncomfortably narrow but, with a few Wild Turkey sours, tolerable.
   D. Unbearable. You would rather drive than fly because the seats are so tight.
   E. Screw the seats. You would rather drive than fly because airplanes are cartridges of death, and only people who don't value their lives take them on a regular basis.
4. You can take a crap in a public restroom if:
   A. There are strangers in the bathroom, but you're in a stall with the door closed.
   B. Only if there's no one in the bathroom.
   C. Only if there's no one in the bathroom or it's someone you know *well.*
   D. You don't ever take a crap in public bathrooms. You wait until you get home.
   E. Anytime anywhere. You could take a crap on a plate in front of your mom.
5. This most closely reflects your view of fate:
   A. Live for now; you could get hit by a truck tomorrow.
   B. Preparing for the future is the best way to ensure happiness.
   C. No matter what you try to do, the result will always be the same. (Or: There is a divine plan.)
   D. It's never too late to change. (Or: I am the master of my destiny.)
   E. You get out of life what you put in.
6. If your bedroom can be seen by the neighbors, you:
   A. Keep the blinds down at all times.

B. Pull down the blinds always before changing.
C. Leave the blinds open except when having sex.
D. Leave the blinds open all the time.
E. Leave the blinds open and spy on the neighbors. Or, close the blinds and spy on the neighbors.

7. When a telemarketer calls during dinner, you:
   A. Listen politely but simmer inside.
   B. Hang up.
   C. Scream at them, then hang up.
   D. Talk to them because you have nothing better to do.
   E. Put them on speakerphone, ignore them and let them talk into the void all they want.

8. When going Greyhound, you can sit this close to the commode without feeling sick:
   A. Within one row. It's fine.
   B. Must be three rows away.
   C. Five rows or more.
   D. Would take the train instead.
   E. Would rather stay home than ride the dog.

9. Your idea of the perfect shower is:
   A. Long and hot, with strong water pressure.
   B. Short and hot, with strong water pressure.
   C. A gentle warm shower.
   D. Jump in, jump out. As long as there's water, it's a shower.
   E. You prefer a bath.

10. Meeting new people is:
    A. A drag.
    B. A thrill.
    C. Sickening.
    D. Not so bad.
    E. Not so bad as long as you can leave whenever you want.

11. Cops:
    A. Are here to serve and protect. You look to them to keep you safe.
    B. Are sometimes a nuisance but make things safer.
    C. Don't really do anything except drink coffee and give people tickets.
    D. Are pigs. The less you see of them the better.
    E. Are your waking nightmare. You are on the lam.

12. How well do you sleep?

A. Like a log. You lie down and you're out until someone shakes you awake.
B. Well. You sleep soundly. You might wake up if there's a loud noise but will fall right back to sleep.
C. Pretty well, but if you're woken up in the middle of the night, it takes a long time to fall back to sleep.
D. Not so well. It takes you a long time to fall asleep, you wake up easily, and then can't get back to sleep.
E. Terribly. You're an insomniac.

SOLUTIONS
Give yourself the number of points you see beside each of your answers.

1. Landlords
A-3   B-4   C-5   D-1   E-2

D, E: Mobile home owners who rent space are the most vulnerable kind of tenants. It's one thing to fight with your landlord and lose your deposit, it's another when you have to take your house with you to leave. It costs over $2,000 to move a double-wide within a 100-mile radius. But with the dog and the lawyer, you're certainly better off.

A: You're probably a pushover. Or a chickenshit. Come on, admit it. How many bottles of Drano do you pour down the hair-clogged tub before you give up and call the landlord?

B, C: You'll be fine.

2. The Ceiling
A-1   B-2   C-4   D-5   E-3

A, B: You have positive ways of looking at a tight situation. The trailer is perfect for you. Though on the isometric front, you may be in danger of breaking some particleboard.

C: The long-suffering, repressed you. You are the kind of person who shouldn't live in a trailer but will insist that you should.

E: Not noticing the roof is fine. But if you are six-two or more, take one point off your score for giving this answer. If you're not a moron already, you will be by the time you finish hitting your head on the trailer doors.

D: Trailers are not for you.

3. Airplane Seats
A-4   B-5   C-3   D-1   E-2

Clearly this defines your need for space and your ability to deal without it. If you chose E, well, who are we to stop you?

4. Public Craps
A-4   B-2   C-3   D-1   E-5

Obviously the less shy the shitter, the better for a trailer. You have the proximity of neighbors, spouses, and the thinness of trailer walls to think about. But shitting on plates is the sign of a true nut. Trailer parks are friendlier to felons than lunatics.

5. Fate
A-5   B-2   C-4   D-3   E-1

To be a good full-timer, you must be a fatalist... You are twice as likely to die on any given day in a trailer home as a regular one, and:

"In tornados, mobile-home residents die at a rate 22.6 times higher than non–mobile-home residents."
—ARKANSAS MOBILE HOME ASSOCIATION

"Mobile-home occupants probably would improve their survival odds in severe storms simply by taking shelter in parked cars."
—KENT STATE RESEARCH

"Fire deaths in mobile homes occur at twice the rate of deaths in 'stick-built' homes."
—U.S. FIRE ADMINISTRATION

6. Privacy
A-1   B-2   C-4   D-5   E-3

Once again, the less shy the better. . . but to a point: Spying on the neighbors might get them all riled up—unless they share your peeping Tom fascination, in which case, watch out. They may be inviting you over for dinner sooner than you think.

7. Aggravation
A-1   B-3   C-4   D-2   E-5

We've all had weird neighbors, but it's best to stay on their good side: The guy who looks like an axe murderer may turn out to be your only ally at a true crisis point. Again, you need a healthy balance between excessive hostility and any sign of meekness. And of course, the ability to ignore things, especially noise, is your primary asset.

8. Smell
A-5   B-4   C-3   D-2   E-1

Some trailers have their own septic tanks, which stink. But even in parks where there is a central tank, the toilets clog more easily because of the low water pressure and thin pipes.

9. Hygiene
A-1   B-3   C-4   D-5   E-2

The less hot water and pressure you need, the happier you will be in a trailer. Long, hard, hot showers are hard to come by. You don't get hot water from a twenty-gallon hot-water heater for very long. And, sorry, most standard double-wides don't have bathtubs.

10. Meeting People
A-3   B-5   C-1   D-4   E-2

Think: Neighbors everywhere, people moving in and out, high unemployment, lots of free time, and little money to go anywhere. Everyone's around all the time, so if you can't hack the folk, get out of the park.

11. Cops
A-1   B-2   C-3   D-5   E-4

Police don't patrol trailer parks regularly, unless they are called in. This is good if you're on the lam, bad if you're looking for help before a crime gets committed.

12. Sleep
A-5   B-4   C-2   D-1   E-3

The only thing that's not so hot about sleeping like a log is if your trailer catches fire. Insomniacs tend to fare better than light sleepers in trailer parks because insomniacs are awake anyway, and at least you might find someone to talk to.

If you got:
49–60 Move on in; you are trailer-true.
37–48 You'll be okay.
25–36 Look before you leap; it's going to be a long, hard fall.
12–24 DO NOT live in a trailer unless you have to. And if you have to, be sure to invest in earplugs and get a prescription of Valium.

T.I.T. #2: Doubling Up

In any relationship, compatibility is key, but the confines of a trailer can put the squeeze on even the closest couple. Can you hack it with a spouse? (Must be taken with potential spouse.)

1. You consider yourself:
   A. A night owl: You're grumpy in the morning.
   B. An early early bird: You get grumpy at night, when you're tired.
   C. Moderate: You get up at a reasonable hour and go to bed at a reasonable hour.
2. When you go on a trip, you:
   A. Plan ahead. You like to know where you're staying and what you're going to see before you get there.

B. Travel by the seat of your pants. It's no fun unless you don't know what's coming.
   C. Would rather stay home.
3. You like to listen to your music:
   A. Loud—all rock and roll all the time.
   B. Quietly. Music should be a soothing background.
   C. A little of both. You're not picky, unless you're trying to go to sleep.
4. You like your house to be:
   A. Clean and well organized.
   B. Controlled chaos. As long as the dishes are clean and nothing's broken, it's home.
   C. You don't care as long as it doesn't stink too much—and you can find the door.
5. You like people to come over:
   A. Often. You throw parties and you like gatherings, all the time.
   B. Sometimes. You like small groups of people to come over, but you also value your private space.
   C. You don't like it. You feel self-conscious when people come over. You'd rather go out.
6. Your TV is:
   A. On much of the time. You love watching sports.
   B. On much of the time, but you hate watching sports.
   C. Off most of time. Having it on too much gets on your nerves.
7. Pets:
   A. Pets are the best. Even strays have a home with you.
   B. You might have a pet or two. They're okay but any more are welcome only if they're visiting.
   C. You're allergic to pets.
8. House Guests:
   A. All the ones you like are welcome for as long as they want.
   B. They're okay, but short visits are best.
   C. You're allergic to house guests.

Solutions: Each of you, add up your score.
1.   A-10   B-0   C-5
2.   A-5   B-10   C-0

3.	A-10	B-0	C-5
4.	A-0	B-5	C-10
5.	A-10	B-5	C-0
6.	A-10	B-5	C-0
7.	A-10	B-5	C-0
8.	A-10	B-0	C-5

To measure your compatibility, subtract the lower score from the higher one. If the remaining number is:

60–80: Forget it. Even in the governor's mansion, you'll be doomed.

40–60: You're more different than alike. It might make the sparks fly, but in the trailer, you're likely to crash and burn.

20–40: It may not be bliss, but you'll make it all right. Just make sure you're not both unemployed at the same time.

0–20: This is clearly a case of like attracts like. You'll do fine in the slimmest single-wide.

TRAILER MODIFICATIONS (MODS)

"We lived in one [a trailer near the army base] where helicopters sometimes blew Tipper's laundry off the clothesline and into the red Alabama clay. Our trailer had a little extension off the living room, and I'm telling you that extra four feet made all the difference in the world. Those were wonderful times."—Al Gore

Just because it's prefabricated doesn't mean a mobile home has to look like everyone else's. There are many simple and effective, even beautiful, ways to customize your trailer. From factory-built add-ons—expandos—which just need to be rolled over and bolted to your "mother unit," to dizzying feats of at-home engineering, trailers can be "worked on" almost as much as your car.

Stilts: Trailer homes on stilts may look more like deranged grasshoppers than home sweet home, but there's a good reason for them. In 1998, following the floods of Hurricane George, the feds ruled that any trailer homes substantially damaged in the Florida Keys must be elevated on stilts. The swamp dwellers of Louisiana seem to have caught on too: In Bayou Pointes Aux Chenes near New Orleans, trailers are perched on twenty-foot poles to stay above the seasonal floods. On Fir Island off Washington state, the Blake family's mobile home has survived seventeen presidential flood disaster declarations over the past twenty years because of its nine-foot stilts.

For those who prefer better visibility without swaying around on a bundle of sticks, there is always "Skyrise," the nation's first multilevel mobile-home park in Vadnais Heights, Minnesota. If you ever decide to pitch up there, drop in on the park prez and tell him we sent you. His name's Elmer.

For those do-it-yourselfers, you can elevate your trailer by building a high platform and hoisting your trailer up there with a crane. You will have the dual benefits of having a better view and blocking your neighbor's. You will have the dual disadvantages of a lowered survival probability during earthquakes and while falling-down drunk.

Double-Wides: The 1950s industry standard for a mobile home was the "single-wide," which was only ten- to twelve-feet wide. Double-wides became all the rage in the 1970s. These twenty-eight-by-seventy-foot homes were first invented in 1955 by Florida's Welburn Guernsey when he bolted two trailers together. He also invented the "landscaped" trailer park, replete with grassy knolls and palm trees.

You can make a double-wide yourself by joining two trailers together: Put them back to back so the back doors open into each other, allowing you to pass from one trailer to the next without going out into the snow. To keep out the damp, build a gutter between the two, along the seam. You can make this gutter with a can opener and a couple of

coffee cans: Cut out the bottoms of the coffee cans, then saw them in vertical halves. Duct-tape them together, and you've got a gutter for your seam.

If your trailer-park plot doesn't allow for lateral homesteading, there is always room for a Missouri favorite, the double-tall: Stack one trailer on top of the other, secure them together with lag bolts, and chop a hole through the ceiling of the bottom trailer and the floor of the top trailer. Stuff a ladder up there, and you have your own split-level home. To keep in the heat and keep out the rain, seal up the crack with insulation and caulk. Some thin aluminum siding wouldn't hurt either.

Get Weird: Some people like to attach their trailer to a boat hull and call it a "troat" (yeah, half trailer, half boat). Why? Because they hope to float away in the next flood? Because they like their boat and don't want to throw it out? Why do people send Fluffy to the taxidermist? Why do they preserve wedding bouquets in silica gel?

Wayne Newton, who in the early nineties filed for bankruptcy, once spent $300,000 renovating his trailer: He built a swimming pool with a wraparound pine deck, a gazebo with a tanning bed, and a hot tub. He then built a road from his trailer to a cave on his property near Ozark, Missouri. To a cave? Why a cave?—Ask Wayne.

Home Stretchers: According to David Nulsen, author of *How to Build Patios, Porches, Carports and Storage Sheds for Mobile Homes*, there are many "rugged additions carefully designed to look like and live like the outdoor facilities found only in the finer residential neighborhoods." Most exotic is perhaps the *carport pergola*, that is, a carport

Macho Mods: In 1972, R. D. Hawkins designed a fiberglass folding houseboat that could double as a camping trailer. But Presley O'Barge, a St. Louis Railroad man, holds the patent for perhaps the most macho mobile home ever dreamed up. Patent number 4,296,892 was granted in 1981 for his spherical mobile home, which, O'Barge says, can rest on the ground, float on water, or fly in the air. If made, this home would come complete with pontoons and helicopter blades—and would most likely cost a few arms and legs.

Mod for the Tall: In 1946 the Liberty Company introduced a unit in which the second story telescoped out from the first. It didn't go into production but was exhibited at the 1947 trade shows. The "pop-up" roof was designed as a solution to the limited headroom inside a trailer. Too bad it didn't take off.

Mod from the Unfriendly Skies: Spartan Aircraft of Tulsa, Oklahoma made 1947's ill-fated "Spartan Manor" out of old World War II airplanes, and insiders reveal that other postwar manufacturers skimped on supplies: They used garden hoses for water supply lines and lamp cords for electrical wiring.

Hot Wings: Not content with a mere Spartan Manor, Bruce Campbell of Hillsboro, Oregon gutted a 727 and, in spite of the "difficulties of getting the damn thing down First Avenue," hauled it into his local trailer park where it became luxury digs.

Tree Trailer: In the '20s, Mr. and Mrs. Wade from the Mississippi Valley set off on a U.S. tour in a mobile home made from the hollowed-out trunk of a 434-year-old fir tree.

Photos by Bruce Campbell (www. AirplaneHome.com)

built in the "Oriental" style with a sloping roof, plaster Fu dogs, and fancy woodwork. A slick trailer trick is to extend your carport over your trailer to provide added protection from the elements. Of course, there are simpler ways to stretch your domain when you don't give a shit about being a fancy pants . . .

The Lazy Man's Porch Attachment: Building a real porch is serious business, but luckily there are ways around it. All you need to do is stack up a wall of cinder blocks flush with your trailer and then extending out to make a sizable square or rectangle. After this, buy some cheap six-by-six pieces of wooden fencing at the hardware store and lay them down flat over the cinder blocks. This creates an authentic wooden porch look and is a great space maker for your washing machine and swamp cooler.

Screw Carports! A well-constructed driveway can do more than be a roost for your car. One West Virginia native hoarded his beer cans all winter and managed to save up enough in recycling to pay his property tax. To crush the cans for recycling he threw them off his trailer porch onto his circular driveway and drove his pickup around and around over them.

SPACE SAVERS

The Murphy Bed: One day, at the turn of the century in San Francisco, William L. Murphy got mad at his bed. The damn thing took up his entire studio apartment. So he found a way to stuff it into the closet, and the Murphy bed was born.

Like the Murphy, in a trailer, anything that folds is your friend. Auto campers of the twenties were experts at foldout devices. One camper had an "autotent" bolted to the running board. It unfolded

> "We lived near the stadium, in a residential hotel. We had a Murphy bed.
> I told him the bed was in the wall and he said, 'I can't sleep standing up'."
> —CARMEN BERRA, RE: YOGI BERRA AND THE 1956 SUBWAY SERIES

automatically into a full-scale shelter with a cot that used the running board itself as a headrest. And a 1920s auto kitchenette carried everything from pots, pans, and stove to ketchup and eggs in a compact box.

Orange Crate La-Z-Boy: The La-Z-Boy was invented by the late Edwin Shoemaker, who lived on a farm outside of Monroe, Michigan. In 1927, he got bored and went to live with a cousin in town, where they experimented building reclining chairs out of plywood and hinges. Eventually they made a folding, reclining porch chair from the slats of orange crates, which became the first La-Z-Boy model. They made the first upholstered indoor recliner in 1929.

THE HOSTEST WITH THE MOSTEST Having a party? Use the fold-away ironing board as a buffet table.

DISGUISES

"The mobile home is not a threat because it is ugly, but because it is identifiably different."—Allan Wallis, *Wheel Estate*

There is a need that flows deep in cracker veins, the need to make a trailer look like something else. Even George Washington himself, though he didn't live in a trailer, had this very urge: What appears to be stone facing on Mount Vernon is, in fact, wood coated with a thin layer of ground-up oyster shells. Just be warned, a poor trailer-disguise job often ends up looking more like the result of a nasty collision than anything else.

The Trouse: The most popular way to disguise your trailer is to make it look like a house. Usually half successful, these dwellings are known as "trouses": half trailer, half house.

In the Southwest, people put plaster over the trailer and porch attachments to make it look like an adobe hut. We've also seen trailers covered with wood, stucco, "form stone" (a Pennsylvania favorite), and fake brick. One of the more obvious ways to make your trailer look like a house is to put a real roof on it. A false chimney nailed to the roof will perfect the illusion. Paint it a convincing color and hope that nobody asks why there's never any smoke.

One giveaway that a trailer is a trailer and not a house is its undercarriage, or chassis. People go through great pains to hide these—and it takes work. You must first set trailer on blocks so it sits two feet off the ground. Then use either large plants or metal skirting to hide the gap. Skirts also block wind and make the trailer floor warmer. To get in, you need to build steps up to the door.

But chassis are a tear in the bucket compared to the challenge that faced generations of trouselings: the problem of the trailer hitch.

Hiding Your Hitch: In 1966, *Trailer Topics* magazine finally addressed the hitch debate. Should you hide it with a bench or planters? And while you're at it, what about planters to cover your propane tanks? Should you view the hitch as a badge of honor? Or should you hack it off? No one could agree. But in the mid-'70s some genius sensitive to the trouseling's greatest need solved the problem once and for all. He invented a hitch that could be *unbolted*.

Trailers aren't just disguised on the outside . . . almost everything in them is designed to look like something else. Trailer manufacturers have perfected the art of almost fooling your eye. This is cracker ingenuity at its finest, and you don't have to lift a damn finger:

- Metal siding has a wood-grain pattern.
- Interior paneling is laminated with photos of decorative hardwoods.
- Ceilings made from foam padding are designed to look like stucco.
- Plastic is made to look like brass, glass, porcelain, and more.

Of course, the true cracker isn't content to let the factory have all the fun. There are many ways to deface or beautify your home, depending on your mood and your precision with a chain saw.

DOORS AND WINDOWS

While you may feel tempted to cut windows in your trailer with a chain saw, we advise you to refrain from doing so, because you're likely to cut through something essential, like electrical wires or a water pipe.

Widening doors with your chain saw is a more viable option. Only be warned, it can get hairy because you'll be cutting through sheet metal, plywood, and fiberglass. Once you cut into the fiberglass, little bits of it will fly around, and you don't want to inhale them. One way to avoid stabbing your lungs with these tiny shards is to put a pair of women's nylons over your head. That way you can both see and avoid breathing in the glass. If this idea embarrasses you, use goggles and a dust mask. When you are done cutting, you will need to plug up the sides of the new door frame. Stuff the sides full of old socks and underwear (wash first). Then, to keep the insulation in place, take pieces of carpet or tough cardboard and use a staple gun to staple them around the door frame.

FLOOR MODS

AstroTurf: AstroTurf makes a cheap carpet that's soft, durable, exceedingly green, and easily hosed off.

Particleboard Parquet: Don't be a chump spending hundreds on hardwood when you can make your own particleboard parquet. Cut small rectangular pieces out of particleboard. Then, slather polyurethane on the floor and lay in your pieces. You will then need to "roll" the floor. You can rent heavy "rollers" for this purpose, but a large kitchen rolling pin works just fine. Get down, put your weight on that pin and roll it across the floor until the parquet holds fast and lies flat.

> **FYI: Particleboard.** This sturdy and very cheap board is a trailer tinker's favorite, and an example of cracker ingenuity itself. Particleboard is an "engineered wood" made up of different recycled woods bonded together with synthetic resins (basically, this means plastic and sawdust). Its ingredients vary according to the types of wood available in a particular region. For example, there's a new type of particleboard on the market in Texas called "bovine board," which is made from cow manure. For more information on the finer points of particleboard, you can call the National Particleboard Association: (301) 670-0604.

SECURITY

"Neighbors are nosy, but it helps with security; they keep their eye on everything."—Pennsylvania trailer park resident

Nobody likes feeling that they're being watched, but the many eyes in a trailer park can deter even the most seasoned thief. If the neighbors' goggling doesn't satisfy your paranoia, it doesn't mean you have to pay through the nose for an electronic burglar alarm. There are always alternatives.

The "Look": There's something to be said for a police lock, but having "the look" is an easier way to keep the robbers out. Say you're a thief, and, as Jeff Foxworthy puts it, "you come up on two houses and one of 'em has a manicured lawn with daisies growing in the flowerpot. You might be thinking, 'Well this is easy pickings.' But you come up on a house where the grass is this tall and there's a dog chained to

---

SUMP-PUMP SHOWER A sump pump keeps leaky basements from flooding by sucking up water and pumping it back out into the yard. But, as one West Virginia native discovered, sump pumps can do more than just drain your floor:

"I remember this pretty ingenious getup that my stepfather, Steve, put together for us out here soon after he arrived in our lives: the Sump-Pump Shower System. I thought it was pretty clever (and told Mom she should keep him). At the time Steve arrived, we did not have running water, and so getting a shower or a bath was a bit of an ordeal. We'd slum showers from friends, heat up water on the stove, and take sitz baths, or use hot tea water and a washcloth for those super fast cleanups. On several occasions we were known to go running wildly into summer downpours with bars of soap in hand. But when Steve arrived, he ran right out and bought a sump pump.

"He put the sump pump in a ten-gallon plastic trash can and attached a garden hose to it and a showerhead at the end of the hose. The pump, can, and plug remained inside the house and was set up with an on-off switch. The showerhead vented into a makeshift outdoor shower setup, that consisted of a couple of boards propped up on cinder block. We'd heat up a big pan of water on the stove to near boiling, and then pour it into the trash can with the pump.

"When all was ready to go, you'd dash out to the shower and yell back to someone waiting for the signal inside that you were ready and your trusty assistant would flip the on switch. When you wanted to end the shower, you flipped another switch out by the shower to turn the pump off. Of course, we used a small stick to hit the switch, so you wouldn't be likely to electrocute yourself."—Kelly Farewell, Hamlin, West Virginia

the clothesline and a motor swinging from the tree . . . Buddy, that's a house where a *gun* lives." (Go to p. 62.)

Clodhopper Deterrent: This is a classic invented by two old ladies immortalized in *Trailer Life* magazine. They leave a pair of size-fourteen boots out on their trailer doorstep at night so that people think a huge man lives there.

K9 and Fowl Patrol: Of course, Man's Best Friend—Rusty, Fang, Sly, Duke, Buddy, and D.O.G.—is often employed as a loyal gate-keeper. But if your dog is prone to fall silent for a handful of hamburger meat, try a few geese. Geese were the guard dogs of ancient Rome. They are said to be more alert than Alsatian guard dogs. And while they may not have six-inch fangs, they make a hell of a racket when disturbed.

Get Serious: Do like they do in northern Florida, and tether a pair of live rattlesnakes to the base of your fence with leather thongs.

Sneaky Creaks: If you've got a slatted porch, loosen a couple of boards until they squeak, so you'll hear even the stealthiest burglar. Creaky stairs are also good for keeping lying teenagers in the house, or at least for catching them when they come home.

PISS OFF!

You don't need a cat to scare off Mickey and Minnie. All you need is to get a wad of feline hair from a cat owner. Sprinkle the hair in the corners of all the rooms in your house and the mice will clear out.

You can also buy fox and wolf piss to spray around your neighborhood. It will scare away small animals and warns the bigger ones that this is someone else's turf.

Tin Can Alarms: Run a piece of fishing line across your front yard so that a prowler will be likely to kick it. One end of the line should be tied around a tree trunk; the other, attached to a cluster of tin cans that hang inside your trailer. When your prowler kicks the line, you'll hear the cans clatter.

Trip Wires: They are not just the residue of Rambo jungle fantasies. Other than detonating a blasting cap into the heart of a massive TNT charge, trip wires can be used to set off fire alarms, turn on the floodlights, or even start the buzzer on your dryer. Run one across your yard, and no one will be able to sneak in without tipping you off. If you really want to dampen the pants of your would-be-intruder, attach the trip wire to a shotgun filled with blanks.

> **FYI:** If you're stashing illegal firearms or drugs in your trailer, watch out. The Supreme Court ruled that although the trailer possesses "some if not many of the attributes of a home," it more "closely resembles" a car, so the cops can search it without a warrant.

MOTHER NATURE

"It's better to wear out than rust out."
—Wally Byam, inventor of the aluminum Airstream trailer

Mother Nature can offer a cold shoulder to those who don't come to the party prepared. While stick-built dwellers enjoy expensive air conditioners and cement basements, trailerites are left to fend for themselves. Luckily, there are ways to prepare.

TEMPERATURE CONTROL

To keep down the heating bills each winter, our friends in Johnson, Vermont, wrap up their entire trailer in industrial clear plastic sheets and duct tape to provide insulation. Except, of course, for the front door. In other pleasant, bucolic settings people put hay bales under trailers to help with insulation. In less pleasant settings, bags of garbage may be stuffed under the trailer to help keep it warm.

When it gets too hot and the air conditioner threatens to eat all your beer money, you can put foil between your windows and screens to reflect heat and sunlight away from your trailer. Or, you can make a swamp cooler.

A swamp cooler is a simple air-cooling device that works by evaporation. These units use far less electricity than air conditioners and can be made at home. A typical swamp cooler is a window-mounted, motor-powered unit with porous pads covering the sides and a blower fan and water pump inside. The pump circulates water into the pads and the fan sucks in the hot outside air, blowing it through the wet pads. Water held by the pads evaporates, and the latent heat of vaporization causes air to cool by as much as twenty-seven degrees. Because it works by evaporation, swamp coolers function best in dry climates like the Southwest.

If your trailer gets *really* hot, however, it's probably on fire.

FIRE

Although there is still a disproportionately high number of fire deaths in trailer parks, there are far fewer than there were before 1974, when new fire codes were introduced. Prior to that, trailers were made from highly flammable and toxic materials, so watch out for old trailers. Otherwise, get a smoke alarm, a fire extinguisher, and sharpen your ax.

HURRICANES

After Hurricane Andrew in August 1992, federal regulations made mobile-home manufacturers build with sturdier materials to ensure that their structures could withstand 110-mph winds. Even so, hurricanes do beastly things to trailers. They will rip off the roof, shatter the windows, splinter the doors, and, once they get inside, they will blow out the walls. So when Hurricane Wanda comes your way make sure you've storm-proofed the trailer. You should bolt particleboard over the windows and use it to reinforce your doors. Also, your roof *must* be anchored to your walls with extra two-by-fours, and the walls *must* be fastened to some sort of foundation if you don't want to be drop-kicked by the storm. As Timothy Reinhold, a wind resistance tester at Clemson, says, "You can build a better box, but it won't make much difference if you don't tie it down."

TORNADOES

Tornadoes are hungry fiends: they've been known to suck up railroad freight cars, telephone poles, and even a huge piece of tarmac off Texas Route 86. They are also picky eaters: Chickens have been literally plucked alive by the winds. A farmer watched from the doorway of his barn while

Find This Man! Carl Shepard holds a U.S. patent for mobile-home fire-escape hatches. The hatch is installed at floor level (below the smoke) and can be put into any trailer wall. It cannot be opened from the outside but is easily popped from the inside. Shepard was in the master machinists division at a General Motors plant in Indianapolis and retired to Florida. He's set up for mass production, but only 2 percent of the 70,000 patents filed yearly make it to the marketplace, so if you're marketing inclined, find this man! And give us a cut of the proceeds.

a tornado carried the rest of it away. A three-year-old girl in Fort Smith, Arkansas, was once picked up by a tornado and set down, unharmed, three miles away. But one thing's for sure: Tornadoes love trailers.

According to the Emergency Preparedness Canada Foundation, more than 50 percent of all deaths from tornadoes occur in mobile homes. They recommend seeking shelter "in a more secure building" when a severe storm approaches, as "trailers are the exception to the stay-indoors rule." In fact, a trailer's structural fortitude is such that the National Weather Service says during a tornado, a person has a better chance of survival by charging outside and jumping into a ditch.

TORNADO SAFETY

If you live in a trailer in Tornado Alley (South Dakota to North Texas via Oklahoma, Kansas, and Nevada), defend yourself:

Build a Storm Cellar: The biggest danger in a tornado is caused by flying objects. For example, a wind of 200 miles per hour can send a 12-foot-long two-by-four flying at 100 mph and you want to be out of the way. Basically, a storm cellar is an underground room, but just about any hole in the ground will do. So dig one.

Bathtubs: A bathtub can provide some shelter in a storm. In one tornado, a woman hid in her bathtub under a blanket. When the storm ended she pulled back the blanket and found herself lying in the middle of the road, unharmed, but her house was completely gone—and so was the bathtub. Because most trailers don't come equipped with bathtubs, we suggest you get one, and look into the "Junkheap Gems" section of this book to discover what you can do with it in between tornado strikes.

Don't Listen to Crackpots: In the fifties, Waco, Texas, residents didn't take the necessary precautions because Indian legend had it that the area was protected from tornadoes. This legend was even printed in Waco's official Chamber of Commerce brochure. But in 1953, a tornado leveled the entire town.

THUNDERSTORMS, ICE STORMS, BLIZZARDS, SNOW, HAIL, SLEET, RAIN

"It sounded like a train coming down the street, but it was trailers hitting other trailers." —Sherry Moore, trailerite, describing a severe thunderstorm in St. Louis

For all sorts of storms you should use tie-downs to secure your trailer to the ground. To stop the accumulation of water on your roof, prop up one end of your trailer with stabilizer jacks, allowing one end to be lower than the other. The water will run off, but you'll have to put up with a tipsy floor.

Also, try to set the trailer back against a natural windbreak like a hill or a stand of trees, and always face the end of your trailer into the prevailing wind so it doesn't get broadsided by a gale. In a storm, horses and cows stand with their rumps facing into the wind for the same reason.

Speaking of the equine and bovine populations, don't be seduced by their big brown eyes; they can inflict significant damage on a trailer. Horny horses and cows love to rub and lean against trailers. Trailer panels can get very badly dented from this and ruin any resale value you might be hoping to have.

EARTHQUAKES

Good news: Earthquakes are one natural disaster where trailer dwellers are at no higher risk of severe injury or death than anyone else.

Wednesday Homes

It's common wisdom that cars built on Wednesdays are least likely to suffer from defects caused by human error on the assembly line. This is because on Fridays the workers want to get on with the weekend, and on Mondays they're still trying to recover from it. The same holds true for mobile homes. At some factories buyers may watch their baby being made, so if you can, watch yourself a Wednesday home.

ALTERNATIVE ENERGY

"If you wrestle with a pig, you'll get dirty and the pig will love it."
—Tim C., ex-Pentagon employee

Why give the electric company and the gas man the satisfaction of being able to shut you off when the bills fall behind, when there are ways around it? Here are some *legal* solutions to the energy crisis.

Engine-Block Oven: Wrap a hunk of meat in aluminum foil and put it in a roasting pan. Open the hood of your pickup and, with a length of wire, secure the pan to the engine block or the exhaust manifold. It takes about 120 miles to cook to well done. The faster you drive, the faster the cooking. With a little preplanning, you can arrive at your relatives' troat with dinner perfectly prepared.

Soda/Brew Cooler: If the mini fridge is too full, try one of these soda/brew coolers to chill your fizz. Like the swamp cooler, the soda/brew cooler works best in arid climates. To make a soda/brew cooler, soak a sock in water, put your can inside, and hook the whole outfit up to the ceiling with a piece of string. You need to hang it so the air makes contact with 100 percent of its surface area. As the water evaporates from the sock, it draws the heat out of your drink.

Bed Warmer: Don't have an electric blanket? Heat some bricks on top of your woodstove, wrap them in old socks, and stick them in your bed. In Victorian times, railroad cars weren't heated, so people would put baked potatoes in their pockets to keep warm. When the potatoes cooled down, they ate them for dinner.

Make Your Own Wood-Burning Stove: A woodstove can be built from a fifty-five gallon drum and lid, depending upon your ability to weld:

"Lay the drum on its side, weld 4 legs on it so it stands a couple of inches off the ground. The legs are just scrap metal you have around. Weld the lid shut. Cut a square door out of the front and put hinges and a latch on it. At the back end of the drum, cut a chimney hole and weld on a regular woodstove flue pipe. Now it's time to put the beast inside and be done with all that expensive electric heat!

The stove cannot be put directly on the floor as it will burn the linoleum, so get some bricks and make a little platform for it. The wall behind the stove needs to be protected too, either with bricks or a piece of reflective sheet metal. If you're smart, you will line the bottom inside of the drum with bricks or sand to get a few more seasons out of it. The metal is thin, and the heat will destroy it after a while.

The last big step is cutting a hole in the side of the trailer wall for the flue. Trailers are always metal on the outside, with a thin layer of insulation and then a thin layer of plywood on the inside: The whole mess of construction is only three to four inches thick. The tool of choice would undoubtedly be a "Sawsall"—the name says it all— and for crude cutting of metal, wood, and fiberglass, nothing can beat it. All carpenters, plumbers, and electricians own one, as any self-respecting man should, I might add."

—Russell Davenport, carpenter, Muncie, Indiana

P.S. If you're a diehard on alternative energy sources, see the "Hard-Core Jerry-Rigs" section for tips on how to tap into high-tension electrical wires. But don't blame us if you end up in the clink.

WASTE MANAGEMENT

After baseball and beer drinking, making trash is America's favorite pastime. Unfortunately for mobile-home residents, they are often not included on municipal garbage routes and not hooked up to the city sewage system, so waste management can be a challenge.

PERSONAL LANDFILL

"If you keep something for seven years, you will find a use for it."—Irish proverb

Some parks provide Dumpsters, and, of course, you can drive your nasties to the dump yourself or chuck them in a field. But if you're wise, you will create your own personal landfill. A personal landfill is not about making new land you can build on but about making a stable junk heap you can build from. As part of the property, your personal landfill is essential for storing trash until you can figure out how to harvest it into something useful.

To create an acceptable personal landfill, you must first acknowledge the difference between biodegradable and nondegradable garbage.

Nondegradable Waste: Plastic, metal, rubber, and any junk that doesn't rot is the mainstay of your personal landfill. Throw it up against a piece of fence to keep it from scattering, and there you go: Out of the way today, material for tomorrow.

Biodegradable Waste: You could try a compost heap, but if you don't want to attract a host of woodland garbage eaters, take it to the dump. Or, make a worm bin under your sink. Here's how:

Put a large, lidded bucket under your kitchen sink. Fill the bottom with an inch or so of sawdust, throw in some worms, and put on the top. Toss potato peels, apple cores, and eggshells into the bin. The worms will feast, pooping out fertilizer for your plants. They will also breed, and you can give them to your friends for Christmas.

SEWAGE

"If it's yellow, let it mellow. If it's brown, flush it down."
—Water-saving axiom

Most trailer parks have "gray" water (dishwater) and "black" water (raw sewage) hookups running into a large septic tank. It's good to know that these kinds of waste pipes are significantly narrower than standard pipes, which means they clog more easily. Some mobile homes have their own underground septic tanks, while others have holding tanks attached to the trailer itself. The holding tank is emptied at a "sanitary discharge station." You can spot this kind of trailer from a mile away because there's a little mushroom-shaped chimney poking out of it. The chimney is there to release the methane—and to tip you off about the impending stink. Of course, there are things you can do with human waste other than clog your septic system:

- Number One: Because urine contains ammonia, and because ammonia is recommended to treat jellyfish stings, various oceanfront medics suggest pissing on the victim's burning flesh. Some old-time ladies also swear that drinking a cup of urine a day will keep you looking fresh as a daisy. Don't try this before a date.
- Number Two: One useful way to dispose of the loaves you pinch is to turn them into nightsoil, that is, fertilizer. It's very effective, but people don't much like the idea of munching on tomatoes grown in human shit.
- Number Three: Horticulture hippies claim that menstrual blood is an unbeatable marijuana fertilizer. Put *that* in your pipe . . .

> **FYI**: A popular fertilizer for golf greens called Milorganite (from Milwaukee) is made from treated sewage.

JUNKHEAP GEMS

"If it ain't trash, it ain't shit."
—Jim Goad, *The Redneck Manifesto*

There are plenty of books out there from back-alley Martha Stewarts intent on showing you how to beautify your crap, so it doesn't look like the crap it is. Books about how to turn a Kleenex box into a jewelry box with varnish, doilies, and a few sequins. Books on how to make birdhouses out of used Popsicle sticks. Books extolling the virtues of pipe cleaners, how to fashion earrings from feathered fly-fishing lures, glue coasters together from old corks, sew pillows from T-shirts, make planters out of melted LPs, do-it-yourself decorating, trash-to-treasure neighborhood fund drives, fun projects, craft-lite, making mosaics from "favorite dishes that get broken"—*throw the shit away.*

There are also numerous tipsters—from Heloise, the *Good House-keeping* "Household Hints" lady, to the authors of your local super handyman column—who are chomping at the bit to help you handle the more practical side of garbage conversion. They can tell you how to make lunch boxes and BBQ starters from paint cans, bottle cork message boards, fire starters from egg cartons stuffed with wax and dryer lint, a strainer out of pantyhose stretched over a coat hanger. How to polish silver and get mold out of tile grouting with toothpaste. And how to make a tennis ball safe or spackle your walls with powdered milk.

Cracker ingenuity, all of it, and God bless. But let's tell the truth.

The most important thing to know how to do with a coat hanger is break into your car, and Thunderbird doesn't come with a cork in it, anyway. But here is some at-home ingenuity of more epic proportions:

CASTLES MADE OF TRASH

PALACE OF DEPRESSION

"The only real depression is a depression of individual ingenuity."
—George Daynor

After having made a fortune in the Alaska gold mines and losing it in the stock market crash of '29, George Daynor wanted to show the world that the Great Depression was beatable. He built the eighteen-spired Palace of Depression in a New Jersey swamp out of mud and rusty car parts. Surviving on squirrels, rabbits, frogs, and ducks, he worked on the palace for three years and completed it on Christmas Day 1932. It soon became known as the strangest house in the world and drew hundreds of tourists. Daynor called one of the rooms the "knockout room" and offered to knock tourists on the head with a bowling ball to get rid of bad memories. When he died, Daynor was supposedly over a hundred, but his individual ingenuity didn't impress everyone: He offered his brain to the Smithsonian, but they declined. A few years later, the palace was burned and dozed over.

WATTS TOWERS

Using a combination of found objects and cement to make walls is a classic cracker move, but possibly the finest example of this kind of work was built by an Italian-born construction worker from Los Angeles. Starting in 1921, Sam Rodia built three towers in his back-

The Watts Towers

yard out of found objects: bed frames, salvaged pipes, cement, bottles, broken glass, plates, and seashells. He worked completely alone and finished thirty-three years later. The tallest of the towers is 99.5 feet high and passed the city's earthquake test.

PARADISE GARDENS

Slowly being reclaimed by the Georgia swamp, Howard Finster's Paradise Gardens is a Pentecostal complex built out of everything you could imagine, including the bones of an unknown girl killed during the Civil War. (She's in a homemade cement coffin, and her teeth show through a tiny glass window.) With chapels made from soda bottle bricks, shrines shingled with broken mirrors, spires of hubcaps and bicycle parts, and a hand-built cathedral, this place is filled with cracker ingenuity, the holy ghost, and kudzu. (Go to p. 62.)

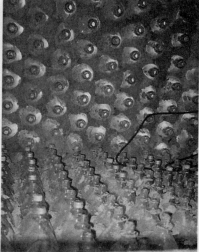

LEFT: *A bottle-brick walled chapel at Paradise Gardens.*

ABOVE: *The interior of a bottle-brick wall at Paradise Gardens.*

SALVATION MOUNTAIN

Shelburne, Vermont, native Leonard Knight saw the light in 1967. He flew a balloon across the country spreading the word. Then, one

day, he landed in the southern California desert and stayed. For the past eighteen years he's been painting the side of Salvation Mountain in praise. Using over eighty thousand gallons of paint, hundreds of hay bales, and homemade adobe, Leonard has created a technicolored mountain. His message: God is love. (Go to p. 62.)

Salvation Mountain. Also on site is a series of enormous buildings, constructed out of hay bales, paint, car windows, and adobe. They are supported by stacks of tires, telephone poles, and sticks made to look like trees (Preceding page, bottom).

GRANDMA PRISBEY'S BOTTLE VILLAGE

"Anyone can do anything with a million dollars. Look at Disney. But it takes more than money to make something out of nothing, and look at the fun I have doing it."—Grandma Prisbey

Grandma Prisbey's Bottle Village in Simi Valley, California, is an entire village made entirely of trash. There are twenty sculptures and thirteen buildings made from thousands of bottles. She started it when she got sick of taking the empties to the dump. And she needed a place to store her collection of over a million pencils.

The Booze Bungalow

BOOZE BUNGALOW

There's a house in Houston, Texas, shingled with beer cans. John Milkovisch started covering his house with beer can skins when he retired in 1968, adding a six-pack a day—which he drank himself—for eighteen years, using about 39,000 cans. He even strung the pull-tabs together to make sun guards for the windows.

THE ORANGE SHOW

Also in Houston, the Orange Show was built by mailman and former orange hauler Jeff McKissak in 1956 as a shrine to the orange. Made out of orange paraphernalia and old wagon wheels, and complete with an amphitheater with seats made from metal tractor seats, it has walls covered with mosaics that read "I love you orange." It is now home of Houston's Art Car Parade (see page 113).

NEWSPAPER HOUSE

In 1922 Ellis F. Stenman made a building material from newspapers by gluing together layers and then putting them under two tons of pressure. The end result was a paper house in Pigeon Cove, Massachusetts, complete with furnishings.

TOP: *The Orange Show.*
BOTTOM: *Iron-wheel fence at the Orange Show.*
RIGHT: *Tractor-seat bleachers at the Orange Show.*

MICHELIN MANSION

Even though tires are thought to have a higher insulation value than any other construction material currently available, there doesn't seem to be much of a market for them. But Vernie Houtchens doesn't mind. He runs a tire graveyard in Colorado, millions of tires strong, and lives in what may be the world's only house made from five-foot-thick recycled tire bricks. In places, the house bulges like the Michelin man, but Vernie doesn't mind that either. In case the look catches on, he has started baling tires from the graveyard: each bale contains a hundred tires, weighs about a ton, and is ready for sale.

"MAN BUILDS DREAM HOUSE FROM 35 TONS OF TRASH"

—*Denver Post* headline, August 2000

Richard Messer built his home from bales of compressed laundry detergent boxes and waterproofed cardboard. The foundation was made from bales of recycled plastic. The house cost $100 per square foot to build (the area's standard is $130 per square foot). Not the biggest bargain, but how many homes can boast a viewing window that shows off the wall's Tide insides?

EARTHSHIPS

Earthships may be homes for hippies, but there's no denying the ingenuity of building houses from tires, bottles, and aluminum cans. Despite their acid-trip origins, earthships have superior insulation and cooling methods. A 2,500-square-foot earthship is made from 3,000 tires and 900 pounds of aluminum cans.

An earthship is built using a combination of "reflecting walls" and "rammed-earth" bricks. Reflecting walls are made from a mixture of cans, glass bottles, and cement. Bottles let light in, while the tin cans

deflect heat. Rammed-earth brick walls are used to support the roof. Rammed-earth bricks are tires filled with earth, which are then tamped down with a sledgehammer. Once these bricks are stacked, they make strong, thick walls with enough "thermal mass" to keep the inside of an earthship nice and cool. This is the same principle behind adobe, which, instead of tires and dirt, uses a mixture of straw and clay to make thick walls.

DEAD VEHICLES AND AMPUTATIONS

Dead vehicles on the property reveal the owner's Ford or Chevy alliance and indicate how long a family has lived there, establishing

their seniority over the neighbors. But they're not only there for stature, they're also there because they're useful.

TRUCK BEDS

- **Swimming Pool:** Line a truck bed with tarp, fill with water, climb in, and drink a beer.
- **Tree House:** An enterprising crane operator in Tennessee lifted his dead 4×4 up twenty feet and wedged it between two trees. It's a neighborhood favorite with the tree-climbing kids, and who's to say it isn't beautiful?
- **Tables:** A tailgate laid across stacked paint cans makes a good coffee table and provides an effective way to demonstrate your Ford/Chevy alliance inside the home.

Truck hoods make a perfect awning for the front door of a trouse.

TIRES

Every year 276 million tires are disposed of (about one per American citizen)—and that's a lot of trash. If Moisture Master can use a million tires a year to make their soaker hoses, what are you waiting for?

- **Signal Fire:** If you ever find yourself snowed in on a road that no one plows during the winter and you don't feel like throwing a Donner party and eating your companions, soak a cloth in the gas tank, use it to set your spare tire on fire, and throw the flaming tire out onto the snow. Tires are made of petroleum, so no amount of melted snow will put them out; they can even burn underground. Your spare will burn for days, huffing out swirls of black signal smoke. So if anybody's bothering to look, they'll find you.
- **Planter:** Stack one tire on top of the other, fill with dirt, and throw in some seeds.

- **Driveway Border:** Cut tires in half, paint them attractive colors, and set them up side by side, like little rainbows, to line your drive.
- **Mailbox Mounter:** Pour cement in the middle of a tire and stick the mailbox post in it.
- **Swing:** Tie it to a rope and hang it from a tree, of course.
- **Shoes:** Cut out a section of the tire the same size as your foot and make straps from duct tape, or tape the tread to the bottom of your worn-out shoes to give them new life.
- **Shock Absorber:** Tires are often used as bumpers on piers, boats, and truck loading bays.
- **Watering Hole:** "Cut a tire in half, crossways, like a bagel, a biscuit or a bread roll. You'll have two separate parts to use as water and feeding bowls for the kitties and pups" (Norm "Nice Guy" Deveraux).

CAR RADIATORS

- **Air Conditioner:** Both car radiators and air conditioners are built on the same cooling principal: the condenser. With a little Freon and a fan, you can convert a radiator into an air conditioner.
- **Van-Powered Hot Tub:** Wood-fired hot tubs have long been the lap of cracker luxury. But sometimes people take it a level beyond . . .

"My friends Dee and Kelly in Reading, Pennsylvania, made a hot tub heated by the radiator in an old van. They constructed the tub out of wood lined with salvaged heavy-duty plastic. Then, they filled the tub with water and ran hoses from the tub to the intake and output of the radiator in the van. When you started the van, the water would run through the radiator and get hot. It took a while to warm up, but it actually worked pretty well.

Leonard Knight's house-truck at Salvation Mountain.

Needless to say, it was not the honey-magnet they envisioned. I got in it once, but the idea of bathing in radiator residue was kind of repulsive. They claimed they cleaned it out, but who knows.

As far as I remember, the whole thing was pretty short-lived. They needed the van for their derby course in the backyard. They built a one-mile racetrack in the backyard and raced old cars around there until they eventually crashed the van into a tree and left it there."

—Cindy "McFly" McTamany

THE WHOLE HOG

- **School Bus Chicken Coop:** In some places it's common practice to keep chickens in the shells of old buses. Or forget the chickens; you can live in the bus, too.
- **Solar Dryer:** To dry hulled black walnuts, spread them in a flat cardboard box, and put them in the back window of a car parked in the sun.

In Northern Nevada there is a town built from cars. And there is Stanley Marsh's Cadillac Ranch in Amarillo, Texas: a row of old Cadillacs stuck nose first into the grass.

LARGE GARBAGE

Junkyard Wars may be a reality TV show these days, but the reality is that people have been creating masterpieces from the junk in their personal landfills for years.

AIR CONDITIONERS

- **Whiskey Still:** Like air conditioners and car radiators, the distillation process depends on a condenser to convert alcohol steam back to liquid. So, the guts of an air conditioner can be used as a condenser in a whiskey still. But a car radiator cannot because radiators are soldered together with lead, which will poison your drink. The question then remains: Can you make a radiator out of an air conditioner?

BEDS

- **Flower "Bed":** Something of a craze in Missouri, people have lately been embedding a headboard and a footboard into the earth and planting a "bed" of flowers in between.
- **Box-Spring Gazebo:** Put three box springs upright, joining the edges together. Top with a plywood roof. Get vines to grow. If you're not feeling this ambitious, you can make a simple trellis out of an old aluminum shoe rack.
- **Bed-Frame Bridge:** Old bed frames can be used as footbridge guardrails.

A bridge guardrail made from an old headboard.

BROKEN TELEVISIONS

Even when the TV tubes are blown, they can still be lovely to look at:

- **Shadowbox:** Smash out the TV screen part, put in baby's first shoes, and then glue on a transparent plastic sheet.
- **Fish Tank:** Saw off top of the TV. Remove the tubes. Caulk all seams. Fill with water and fish.

OIL DRUMS

They're everywhere—in old dockyards, by railway tracks, in vacant lots and toxic waste dump sites (Warning: Toxic!)—and can be used for more than a wood-burning stove.

- **Bum Fire:** To keep a fire going in a drum it's essential to pierce some holes in its sides so the fire gets enough oxygen.

Farmers use this kind of oil drum fire—a.k.a. smudge pots—in their fields during cold weather to keep sensitive crops like oranges and grapes from freezing.

- **Outdoor Shower:** Bolt an oil drum up on the edge of a low, angled roof, where it will collect rainwater. Solder a pipe to the oil cap and attach a handle and a showerhead. When the drum is full of water, just turn the handle.

- **BBQ Pit:** Cut the drum in half, mount on a metal stand, fill with coals, and put a grill on top. Or you can fill an old metal wheelbarrow with coals, lay your grill on top, and use that instead.

WIRE SPOOLS

- **Picnic Table:** These industrial-sized spools are made of wood and they roll, so they're easy to steal. They make the perfect picnic table, complete with a hole for the umbrella. They're also useful for building an electricity-tapping device (see page 59).

WOOD PALLETS

- **Fence:** Wooden pallets can be stood on their sides for a Tom Sawyer–style picket fence.

OVENS

- **Shed:** An old oven makes a great waterproof/animal-proof storage shed. No modification required.

REFRIGERATORS

- **Keggerator:** Even when a fridge gets too scuzzy to keep your steaks fresh, it can still keep your beer kegs cold. Many of the nation's finer beer outlets sell keggerator kits, which are simple to install. Basically all you need to do is cut a hole in the fridge door and attach a tap. Then you run a hose from the tap to a CO_2 tank to keep up the fizz, and then run the CO_2 tank to your keg, which stays peacefully cool inside the fridge. (Go to p. 62.)
- **Smoker:** Chisel vents into the top of an old fridge and build your fire at the bottom. Hickory and cherry are the best woods for smoking. To make a meat rack, punch holes in the sides of the fridge and push rebar through. You can include a rack of wire mesh inside for your mullets.
- **Coffin:** Not the most glamorous of eternal resting places, but a fridge will definitely keep the worms out.

BOILERS

- **Whiskey Still:** There are endless cracker variations on the whiskey still, but using a boiler to house your condensing unit (coils of copper pipe) has an advantage over the fifty-five-gallon drum: It has a built-in pressure gauge that will let off steam before the whole thing blows to pieces.

BATHTUBS

Since most trailer bathrooms don't have one, an old bathtub can be used as a bathtub if you don't mind taking your bath in the front yard. And, of course, on Superbowl Sunday, fill it with ice and a load of beers, and you're good to go. Using a tub for your beers instead of a keggerator has the disadvantage of needing ice but also means you'll have the tub on hand when the tornadoes strike. Bathtubs can also be used to make:

TORPEDO RIDES

In the sixties, proud grandpa Bill Koheler made rides for his grand-kids out of junk. He built a merry-go-round out of World War II torpedoes and a Ferris wheel out of junkyard lumber. "Once I was in an army surplus store and saw some empty bomb shells," Koheler said. "To me, however, they looked like little rocket

ships, and I decided they would make a good merry-go-round for the children to play on." Nice vision. Why did he do it? "I get so excited, I can hardly wait to see the children's faces when my work is finished," he said. Not that a daisy cutter is necessarily what you want for a space shuttle, but this man had the right idea.

Top: *Bill Koheler's torpedo merry-go-round.* **Bottom:** *Bill Koheler's Ferris wheel.*

- **Fish Pond:** Fill it with water and little orange fish.
- **Kiddie Pool:** Fill it with water and little children.
- **Fountain:** Get yourself a water pump and a hose. Plug up the drain of your tub. Then, attach the pump to the hose, drop the pump into the water, and plug it in. Water will spurt up out of the hose, making a jet fountain. For a different look, stick the hose through the mouth of a gnome, cement titmouse, or some other garden creature, and let the water cascade back down into the tub.
- **The Works:** Fill your fountain with little orange fish and children.
- **Garden Shrine:** Turn the tub on end, embedding the faucet end deep into the dirt so that the faucet, taps, and plug hole are hidden below ground but the other end rises into the air. Put a statue of Christ or the BVM in it.

- **Booby Trap:** If you're a guerrilla type, you can protect your flank or a hole in the fence with a good bathtub trap. Sink the tub into the ground and cover it with some thin boards and a bunch of grass and weeds. A trespasser falls right through into . . . cold water? battery acid? raw sewage? You decide.

SINKS

- **Birdbath:** Plug it up, fill it with water, and watch the fowl play. For a classic Greco-Roman look, train vines to twist and twine around the standing sink shaft.

TOILET BOWLS

- **Planter:** For a distinctive planter, fill the bowl with soil and night soil, and soon it'll be pushing up daisies. (Pickle barrels, truck beds, and hollowed-out tree stumps should also be considered viable planter candidates.)

For the "Bathroom Ensemble" look, put your sink birdbath, tub fountain, and toilet bowl planter out together on the lawn. Eat your heart out, Martha.

HARD-CORE JERRY-RIGS

Okay, we're not saying this is all honorable, but it is part of the jerry-rig scene and we'd be leaving a piece of the truth behind if we left it out.

STEALING ELECTRICITY

"It's the only industry I know . . . where the cash register is on the customer's property."—Howard Dean, PG&E revenue protection specialist

"This is dangerous and if you get caught you'll have zero cash for a long time and you might blow your balls off too while you're at it."—"W," professional electricity poacher

METER CHEATERS

The way most people steal their electricity is by cheating the meter to make it read lower than it should. But to do this without ending up in court, "W" says you have to be clever.

Magnets: Sometimes, "W" puts a large speaker magnet up against the glass to slow the disc down.

- **Plus:** It's not necessary to break into the meter and the magnet can be taken away, leaving no evidence for the meter man.
- **Minus:** It doesn't slow it that much, and it doesn't always work.

Piano Wire: Other times, "W" drills a small hole through the meter glass at the same level as the turning disc but on the side of the meter, so it's not easy to see. Then he jams a piece of piano wire up against the disc, to stop it completely.

- **Plus:** Because the meter stops completely, it's easy to control the reading, and the wire is removable.
- **Minus:** If the wire is forgotten or left on for too long, the reading will dip too low, making the meter man suspicious. And if he is suspicious and checks the meter carefully, he will find the hole. (Caught! Go to p. 190.)

Sugar and Flies: For a more organic effect, "W" drills a tiny hole in the top of the meter box and pours in syrup to attract insects. Little fruit flies and the like find their way inside, stick on the wheel and slow it down.

- **Plus:** The meter man will probably be too grossed out to look for the hole.
- **Minus:** The meter is in the house, and so are the flies.

Turn the Meter Upside Down: When it's necessary to reduce the meter reading after the fact, "W" snips through the wire on the lead seal on the meter case, opens the glass, and turns the meter upside down. This makes the meter run backwards. After running it backwards for a while, "W" flips the meter back over and puts the seal back on and hides the snip so that it looks like no one ever touched it.

- **Plus:** It's possible to reduce the reading after the fact, and not necessary to drill through the glass.
- **Minus:** If the meter is left upside down for too long, it's possible to get a negative reading which will give you away. And if the meter man looks, he will be able to find the snip in the seal wire. (Go to p. 190.)

Distracting the Meter Man: One lady in Riverdale, Georgia says she makes sure she's always in her "little nightie" and burning "bacon in a dirty pan to get the place filled with smoke. I even get the fire alarm going too, on occasion." When the meter man comes, "he never does get a good look" (at the meter). Point taken. "W" says the keys to meter messing are (1) never to take too much and (2) keep the meter man from paying close attention to the meter when he comes by.

Dogs: Others opt for sheer intimidation: Rusty, Fang, and Duke can be used to keep the meter man away from the box altogether.

Idiot Box: The Long Island Lock-Picker

In the eighties, the infamous Long Island Lock-Picker did meter rollbacks in diners across Long Island for five years, stealing electricity worth $1.2 million and making up to $150,000 a year for his services. He designed special tools to pick through the meter locks and seals and to reattach wires without leaving a trace. Even after the Lilco Security Department became suspicious and started snooping around, they couldn't detect his tampering. The lock-picker was caught only after trying to break into a house for a regular burglary, and, unfortunately for him, someone was home and called the cops.

On the lock-picker's person, the police found his meter tools and a log detailing all the rollbacks he had ever done. To get off, the lock-picker cooperated with feds, helping bust forty-four people. But afterward, of course, he had to flee Long Island fearing for his life.

FYI: People growing pot often steal electricity to do it. So much so that cops regularly track stolen electricity records to locate grow houses. (Go to p. 190)

"I Forgot": One bill evader has a method he claims works for months: stall paying your bill until the electric company threatens to shut your power off. Then send them the bill with the "amount paid" stub filled in for the whole amount, but no check. Don't seal the envelope. When the company calls you, say you mailed the check, but it must have fallen out. Promise to send another check after the stop payment of the original goes through. They'll wait for the next check. Eventually, they will shut you down and while you won't be winning any friends, you might be able to your stall your way though the winter.

Billing Under a False Name: Rather than just not paying and waiting for the electricity to get shut off, some people feel better about themselves by billing under a false name and waiting for the electricity to get shut off. One electric company admits to billing a "Mr. U. Ben Hadd."

Extension Cords: Sometimes unloving neighbors will steal electricity from each other by plugging extension cords into each other's exterior sockets, or by tying into each other's power lines, but luckily, there are ways to protect yourself:

Catch As Catch Can!: Find out if your neighbors are stealing electricity from you: Wait until they get home and turn on their lights. Throw all your breakers. Your lights will go out, but see if anybody else's do. If your neighbors' lights go out, you've got them. If not, it doesn't mean they're not using your power, just that they're not stealing it with anything visible, so go check your meter. The meter should have come to a complete stop. If it hasn't then you can be reasonably sure that someone is stealing from you—but who?

TIE-INS AND BYPASSING THE METER

"It's not easy to do for someone just trying to be an anarchist."
—David Loeb, electrician

People who don't have a disc meter or are too macho to mess with it, sometimes tie-in to the power lines directly, bypassing the meter. "Tie-in" means to run one line of electricity off another, and is something which can easily get you zapped, because you need to attach your cables to the source electricity cables while they are live. There are always three wires (hot, neutral, and ground) involved in any line, which makes tying in more complicated because it is essential that you attach your clips to the ground wire first, then the hot to avoid frying. Construction and film crews sometimes legally tie-in to power their equipment, and they are highly trained to do so. Even so, the film electrician's manual also recommends that when you tie-in, you should have someone standing by with a piece of wood to smack you with to knock you off the wire when you accidentally get zapped. Worth the risk? Hardly. But even so, it is done and can be done in many different ways: "You think of it, we've seen it," says Leo Dalbec, of National Grid-USA. (Go to p. 62.)

GAS METERS

Gas meters are hard to mess with. They're usually positive displacement meters, which measure precise volumes of gas as it passes through the meter, without relying on a mechanical counter. If you slow or stop the meter, you will slow or stop the gas too. And because gas behaves nothing like electricity, tying into a gas main is very difficult to do and has a high risk of leaking explosive gas. Even so, people have been known to do it using bicycle inner-tubes or garden hoses. (Go to p. 62.)

CABLE

For years, people have been devising ways to get more channels on the boob tube without paying for them. People buy pirated cable boxes and link multiple TVs to one line using co-ax cables to split the signal. This is illegal. (Go to p. 190.) Or they buy basic cable and find ways to trick the TV into giving up the premium channels. This may not be illegal, but it doesn't always work.

The Mad Scientist Way

In *Back to the Future* Christopher Lloyd and Michael J. Fox harnessed the power of a lightning bolt, but that was a movie. There is one equally strange way to nab electricity without connecting directly to any wires. But how much you get depends on how close you are willing to live to the source.

You have to roll a large wooden spool holding several thousand feet of 12 AWG copper wire directly beneath some high-tension power wires carrying something like 600 volts. Now that's a spooky amount of electricity—a single zap will kill you. Electricity bleeds naturally off these mother wires—which is also spooky. Film crews shooting in the desert beneath high-tension wires have reported getting shocks from just touching their metal cameras. If you get your copper close enough, it will conduct the leaking electricity, and you can run it into your house. (If you put your spool close to the third rail of an electric train track, the effect would be similar.) By decreasing the distance between your spool and the wires, you increase your power. This kind of power is unregulated and prone to surges, so you run the risk of either not getting enough or blowing all your electrical equipment, but it's still out there. Maybe those people who claim they pick up radio frequencies in their tooth fillings are actually telling the truth.

PREMIUM CHANNELS

Cleaning Garbage: Many channels don't scramble their signal; they just transmit garbage, or "noise," at the same frequency, so when you tune in with basic cable (but don't have the premium movie channels) you get both the picture and the snow to cover it up. If you can almost get a picture on one of these channels by fine tuning, or if the picture is lined and flashing, you can usually get it to clear.

Fine-Tune with a Three-Part Antenna: Get a three-foot piece of antenna wire, strip one end, and attach it to the VHF terminal on your TV along with the cable. Tune to the desired channel and adjust the antenna, trimming it as necessary to get the best possible picture (should be significantly better than it looks without the antenna). Take a piece of aluminum foil and wrap it around the antenna wire. Slide it up or down until you get a good picture.

CHANNELING

A native of Rock Hill, South Carolina, fashions "homemade cable TV antennas" from wire, electrical tape, and hubcaps. He also uses Coke cans attached to radio antennas for better reception and has made a helmet with a radio antenna attached to it so that he can "listen in." But listen in on what, exactly?

Magnet Box: Put a bar magnet on the bottom of the cable box. Tune to the desired channel and move the magnet slowly around on the bottom of the box until you get a perfect picture (make sure it's the station you were trying to get). This should make all the other garbage channels clear, too. The drawback to this method is that it can mess up your cable box in the long term, and the cable company surely won't give you another one.

Scrambled Premium Channels: No matter what you do, some channels will not come up because their signal is actually scrambled and must be unscrambled at the main cable box before you can see it. There is only one way to get unscrambled channels, and that is to go to the source. One charming cable poacher left these words of advice on the Internet: "It is very important you do this when no one is outside, otherwise your plan will be ruined. Go outside. Find where your cable relay is. Not the one on your house, dork, but the one in your alley, telephone poll (sic), backyard, frontyard (sic) or near your house. The *box* type cable relay is usually green or gray . . . find a way to break the lock on the cable box. OK James Bond, your operation is to remove the little silver-looking tubes. These tubes block out (premium) channels. Take off one of the little tubes. Close box, go inside, turn on your TV to see which channels the Lucky Charm Leprechaun left you. OK, you keep removing them until you have every single pay channel imaginable. There is one problem with this plan, next time the cable man comes by and sees you have been ripping off over $50 worth of pay channels every month, he is going to be pretty pissed off." (There's another problem: Go to p. 190.)

OFF THE GRID

Living "off the power grid" completely means not being connected to any public utilities at all: no gas, no electricity, and no phone. To most, this screams extremist, but it really is the most legal way to keep expenses down. And it doesn't mean you have to live in the dark, just that you must come up with your own power supply (see p. 216). So go out there and do it. And don't come back.

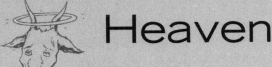

Heaven

"When Jesus left this earth he sent us the Holy Ghost, which was the last thing from God to all people on earth. And there won't be anything else given. Where by that we can be saved by, it is God's last offer."
—REVEREND HOWARD FINSTER

RESIDENTS

There may not be a lot of cracker ingenuity required once you're in heaven, but it sure can be useful beforehand when you're getting in touch with the Holy Ghost.

1. Hank Williams, Sr.

2. The Reverend Howard Finster started building Paradise Gardens in 1961 as a meditation place. He had a vision: "In 1976 he was rubbing paint on a bicycle with his fingers and saw the image of a face on the end of his finger. He had a vision. A voice told Howard to do sacred art. He replied that he could not do art because he was not a professional. The voice asked him repeatedly, 'How do you know?' The Reverend Howard Finster has followed his vision and the image of the face on his finger" (Beverly Finster, Howard's daughter).

3. _____

4. _____

5. _____

GETTING GOD'S ATTENTION

Commandments: The Fields of the Wood in Murphy, Tennessee, holds the "World's Largest Ten Commandments"—a 300-foot-wide tablet built in 1945 on a mountainside by the Church of God of Prophecy, who claim that it can be seen from outer space.

Christus Gardens in Gatlinburg, Tennessee, is one of the world's only religious theme parks.

Buckshot Bible Fortunes: It may be mixing beliefs, but it's cheaper than a Tarot read: On the Fourth of July in the Texas Panhandle, people tell their fortunes by shooting at Bibles nailed to fence posts. They then open the bullet-peppered Bible and read the verse at the indentation on the page where the slug came to a stop and consider it to be their fortune for the coming year.

Food

Much cracker fuel is found at Arby's and Mickey D's, and clearly there is no original value meal quite like a MoonPie and a cold Royal Crown Cola. But for those who cook at home, the cracker kitchen is a place where singular magic happens and cans of food are transformed into things they clearly are not. After all, what is alchemy if it's not being able to make apple pie without apples? Fudge from cheese? Cake from Coke? Betty Cracker knows all the transformational properties of prepackaged, pre- served foods. And it doesn't stop at the table: She's got beauty secrets too. But no, she's not going to tell you how to cook roadkill.

BETTY CRACKER

"Just becasue Pillsbury crescent rolls come in triangles, doesn't mean you have to use them in triangles."

—Demorge Brown, Port Arthur, Texas

APPETIZERS

PIG NEWTONS

1 can SPAM
1 can Pillsbury crescent rolls

Cut the SPAM loaf in half, then cut each half into ¼-inch thick slabs. Unroll the crescent rolls and separate into 2 long rectangles. Pat the remaining perforations in the dough closed. Arrange the SPAM slices end to end down the middle of each rectangle. Bring the sides of the dough up over the SPAM and seal closed. Turn over and slice into 1-inch sections. Place on a cookie sheet. Bake at 350° F for 15–20 minutes, until golden brown.

A Word on SPAM

"Does SPAM taste corpsy? Of course it tastes corpsy—it's meat. We're just arguing about the identity of the deceased." —CECIL ADAMS, *The Straight Dope*

SPAM has captured the imagination of the Internet generation as a great cracker icon, and it's getting a little old. I mean SPAM's all right, but to have not one but two warring cook-offs, the Spamjam in Mississippi and Spamarama in Texas? Gold SPAM-can earrings? SPAM milkshakes? SPAM and Jell-O pudding pie? SPAM martinis? Come on, it's spiced ham. What's the big deal? How come no one has a Web site shrine for Rose's Pork Brains in Milk Gravy?

LITTLE GEM COCKTAIL WEENIE

10 ozs. grape jelly
10 ozs. chili sauce
2 tbsp. cornstarch
1 large pkg. cocktail weenies

Mix jelly, chili sauce, and cornstarch in a little saucepan. Cook over medium heat, stirring often, for 5 minutes until thickened.

Heat weenies. Combine with sauce and serve in warming dish with fancy toothpicks.

GOLD DIGGER'S FONDUE

1 large jar Cheez Whiz
1 cup beer
Dash of garlic powder

Melt together and serve with crackers or potato chips.

BEER SOUP

1 can condensed tomato soup

1 can condensed green pea soup

1 can beer

1 cup milk

Combine ingredients in a pot and heat *without* boiling.

ENTRÉES

HAMBURGER PIE

1 lb. ground beef

½ medium white onion

2 servings instant mashed potatoes

1 can Pillsbury crescent rolls

1 16 oz. can pork and beans

1 cup grated Cheddar cheese

Brown the beef and onion in a skillet.
Make the mashed potatoes. Unroll
the crescent rolls and fit rectangle
into a 9-inch pie pan to make the crust.
Make the first layer of the pie with the beef mixture, then add a layer of potatoes, then a layer of pork and
beans. Top the pie with cheese and bake at 300°F for 15 minutes.

HOT DOG PIE

1 package corn bread mix

½ cup water

1 16 oz. can chili

PAM cooking spray

6 hot dogs

Combine corn bread mix and water; fold in chili. Spray 10-inch pie pan with PAM. Pour in the corn bread mixture and arrange hot dogs attractively on top. Bake at 375°F for 20 minutes.

TATER-TOT CASSEROLE

1 lb. lean ground beef
1 medium onion, chopped
1 can mushroom soup
1 tsp. Worcestershire sauce
Salt and pepper
1 (32-oz.) pkg. Tater Tots
1 cup grated Velveeta cheese

Brown beef and onion in skillet. Drain and mix in soup and Worcestershire sauce. Add salt and pepper to taste. Pour mixture into a buttered casserole dish. Top with Tater Tots. Sprinkle with cheese. Bake at 350°F for 50 minutes.

ETHNIC FOOD

Mexican: TACOS

4 small bags Fritos
1 16 oz. can chili
1/2 cup grated Cheddar cheese
Squeeze the bags of Fritos (without opening) to crush the chips. Heat up the chili. Open the Frito bags, and pour in the chili over the Frito crumbs. Sprinkle the cheese over the chili. (Optional: add diced tomatoes and shredded lettuce.) Eat straight out of the bag.

Italian: LASAGNE

6 ozs. lasagne noodles

1/4 tsp. oregano

1 (16-oz.) jar spaghetti sauce with meat

1 cup cottage cheese

1 cup shredded cheese (any kind will do)

Cook noodles. Then, in a greased baking dish, make layers in order, using half of each of the different ingredients. Noodles should be layered first, then the cottage cheese, then the regular cheese, then the spaghetti sauce, and finally the oregano. Repeat and bake at 375°F for 30 minutes.

Chinese: CHOW MEIN CASSEROLE

1 can condensed cream of mushroom soup

1/4 cup water

2 cups chow mein noodles

1 can tuna

1/2 cup cashew nuts or peanuts

1/2 cup diced white onion

1 cup sliced celery

Combine soup, water, and half of the noodles, then blend in the remaining ingredients, except noodles. Transfer mixture to buttered baking dish. Sprinkle the remaining half of the noodles on top of the casserole and bake at 375°F for 30 minutes.

Indian: SEAFOOD CURRY

2 servings Minute rice

1 can condensed cream of chicken soup

1/2 cup milk

1 tsp. curry powder

1 cup canned imitation crabmeat

Make Minute rice. Mix soup, milk, curry powder, and crabmeat in a skillet. Heat up, and serve over rice. Throw in some raisins and peanuts for extra authenticity.

SNACKS

IRONED CHEESE SANDWICH

Take 2 slices of Wonder bread and spread them with butter. Put some cheese in between, wrap the sandwich in tinfoil, then take out your iron and ironing board. Iron that sandwich and iron it good. Pretty soon the cheese will melt, and when you unwrap it, you'll find that the bread is golden brown.

MEAL ON THE RUN

Drop salted peanuts into a bottle of Coke. Drink the soda and slurp out the peanuts.

DESSERTS

VELVEETA FUDGE

$\frac{1}{2}$ lb. Velveeta
1 cup (2 sticks) margarine
2 lbs. powdered sugar
$\frac{1}{2}$ cup cocoa
1 tsp. vanilla extract
$\frac{3}{4}$ cup chopped nuts

Melt cheese and margarine in a saucepan over low heat. Sift sugar and cocoa into the saucepan, stirring continuously. Stir in vanilla and nuts. Pour into buttered pan and refrigerate overnight. Cut and serve.

MOIST CHOCOLATE MAYONNAISE CAKE

2 cups flour
1 cup sugar
⅓ cup cocoa
2 tsp. baking soda
⅛ tsp. salt
1 cup mayonnaise
1 cup water, at room temperature
1 tsp. vanilla extract

Sift together dry ingredients. Add mayonnaise, water, and vanilla; stir until smooth. Pour batter into greased and floured 9-inch round cake pan and bake at 350°F for 25 minutes.

TOMATO SOUP SPICE CAKE

½ cup (1 stick) butter or margarine
1 cup white sugar
1 egg
1 can tomato soup
2 cups flour
2 tsp. nutmeg
2 tsp. cinnamon
1 tsp. ground cloves
2 tsp. baking powder
1 tsp. baking soda
¼ tsp. salt
½ cup walnuts
½ cup raisins

Cream the butter and sugar together. Mix in egg and tomato soup, until smooth. Sift together flour, spices, baking powder, baking soda, and salt. Stir the dry ingredients into the batter. Mix in the walnuts and raisins. Pour into a greased loaf pan and bake at 350°F for 1 hour.

NO-BAKE ICEBOX CAKE

There are two classic ways to make this no-bake cake:

RECIPE #1

1 pkg. Nabisco's Famous Chocolate Wafers
1 container Cool-Whip

Frost cookies on one side with Cool-Whip. Stack the frosted cookies against each other, making an endless "Oreo" log. Keep stacking until all the cookies are in the log. Cover whole log with remaining Cool-Whip. Freeze for 1 hour. When serving, cut pieces on a diagonal to show off the black and white stripes.

RECIPE #2

1 small pkg. chocolate pudding
8 whole graham crackers

Make the pudding according to package directions. Break up graham crackers. Starting with the graham crackers, alternate layers of graham cracker and pudding in a 9 × 5-inch loaf pan, working quickly so the pudding doesn't set up. You should have enough for three layers. Refrigerate for 2 hours.

KETCHUP APPLE CRUMBLE

⅓ cup tomato ketchup
2 tsp. lemon juice
6 cups (about 2 lbs.) peeled, cored, and sliced tart cooking apples
⅔ cup flour
⅓ cup granulated sugar
1 tsp. cinnamon
⅓ cup softened butter or margarine

Blend ketchup and lemon juice. Combine with apples. Put in deep baking dish. Mix flour, sugar, cinnamon, and butter together. Sprinkle mixture over apples. Bake at 425°F for 40–45 minutes, or until apples are cooked.

GRITS PIE
1 cup quick-cooking grits (cooked)
1 cup brown sugar
2 tsp. flour
2 large eggs, lightly beaten
4 tbsp. milk
2 tbsp. margarine, melted
1 tsp. pure vanilla extract
1 tsp. white vinegar
1 (9-inch) pie crust, unbaked

Make grits according to package directions. Combine grits, brown sugar, flour, and eggs. Mix well, then stir in the milk and margarine. Add vanilla and vinegar; mix well. Pour filling into the pie shell. Bake at 350°F for 35 to 40 minutes, or until the center is just set. Serve warm.

NO-NUT PECAN PIE
2 eggs, beaten
1 cup sugar
1 cup maple syrup
1 cup quick-cooking oats
1 cup sweetened, flaked coconut
1/3 cup margarine, melted
1 (9-inch) pie crust, unbaked

Combine all the ingredients, except the crust, in a mixing bowl; mix until well blended. Pour filling into pie shell. Bake at 400°F for 45 to 50 minutes. Cool thoroughly before cutting.

LIME-AID PRETZEL PIE

1¼ cups crushed pretzels
1 tbsp. sugar
½ cup (1 stick) butter, melted and cooled
6 tbsp. frozen limeade concentrate (thawed)
1½ tsp. grated lime rind
6 cups vanilla ice cream (softened)

Combine pretzels, sugar, and butter; mix well. Press mixture over bottom of pie plate: Freeze for 1 hour. Blend the remaining ingredients; press into the frozen shell. Freeze for several hours. Serve.

BEER MILK SHAKE

1 cold beer
1 scoop vanilla ice cream
Chocolate syrup

Blend together, pour, drink (a great disguise for drinking beer in the middle of the day).

POTATO CHIP COOKIES

½ cup (1 stick) butter, softened
1 cup sugar
1 cup crushed potato chips (preferably Munchos)
3½ cups flour
2 tbsp. vanilla extract

Cream butter and sugar. Add remaining ingredients; stir until blended. Roll dough into little balls, flatten, and bake at 325°F for 12 minutes.

PUDDING AND PANCAKE COOKIES

1 pkg. instant pudding, any flavor
¾ cup Bisquick
¼ cup oil
1 egg

Mix ingredients together. Drop by spoonfuls onto baking sheet. Bake at 350°F for 15 minutes.

BACON AND EGG COOKIES

Powdered sugar
Water
1 pkg. straight pretzel sticks
Yellow M&Ms

Mix powdered sugar and water to make a thick, pasty icing. Place 2 pretzel sticks side by side. Put a blob of the icing on the 2 pretzels so they stick together. Put a yellow M&M in the middle of your blob of icing. The end result should look like a fried egg on 2 strips of bacon. Refrigerate 30 minutes until icing has set.

GIRL SCOUT RIP-OFF COOKIES

1 lb. chocolate chips
1 ¾ tsp. peppermint extract
24 Ritz crackers

Melt chocolate. Add extract. Dip crackers in chocolate to coat them. Chill on waxed paper.
They taste like thin mints.

THREE-COURSE IMPOSTOR DINNER MENU
(Surf 'n' Turf)

APPETIZER: Fishy "Shrimp" Cocktail

(1-lb. pkg.) jumbo pasta shells
2 cans tuna, drained and flaked
1 tbsp. finely chopped scallion
1 stalk celery, diced
⅔ cup mayonnaise
Dash of salt
Cocktail sauce

Cook pasta with a drop of oil until cooked but still firm (al dente). Drain and allow the shells to cool. Mix the tuna, scallion, celery, mayonnaise, and salt together. Stuff each shell with a tablespoon of the tuna mixture. Hold shells closed with a toothpick. Chill and serve with cocktail sauce.

ENTRÉE: No-Calf Cutlet

Thick-cut baloney slices (each should be about ¼ inch thick)
3 eggs, beaten
A mixture of breadcrumbs and crushed cornflakes
Mazola oil

Dip each baloney slice into the egg, then coat with the breadcrumb and crushed cornflake mixture. Heat the oil in a skillet until hot but not smoking. Put in the baloney slices; cook until lightly browned. Place slices on a paper towel to drain. They should resemble breaded veal cutlets.

SIDE DISH: Mock Potato Casserole

6 slices Wonder bread

6 slices Velveeta

2 tbsp. butter, melted

Layer bread and cheese into a casserole dish. Pour melted butter over top. Bake at 350° F for 30 minutes. Serve instead of scalloped potatoes.

DESSERT: Cracker Apple Pie

(No Apples Required)

1 (9-inch) pie crust with top, unbaked

36 Ritz crackers, coarsely broken

   (1¾ cups crumbs)

1¾ cups water

2 cups sugar

2 tsp. cream of tartar

2 tbsp. lemon juice

Grated peel of 1 lemon

½ tsp. ground cinnamon

2 tbsp. butter

Fill crust bottom with cracker pieces. Heat water, sugar, and cream of tartar to a boil; simmer 15 minutes. Add lemon juice, lemon peel, and cinnamon; take off heat. Melt in butter. Cool. Pour cooled syrup over cracker crumbs. Put on crust top; seal and slit. (If you don't have a crust top, use a layer of saltine crackers.) Bake at 425° F for 30 minutes, until crisp and bubbly.

WASH IT DOWN WITH SOME: Sneaky Ginger Ale

Bartenders have been doing this for years: If you run out of ginger ale, just mix Coca-Cola and Sprite or 7-UP in equal parts.

RC COLA CAKE

2 cups flour
2 cups sugar
1½ cups mini marshmallows
½ cup Crisco
½ cup margarine
3 tbsp. cocoa powder
1 cup RC Cola
½ cup buttermilk
1 tsp. baking soda
2 eggs, beaten

Sift together flour and sugar, then add marshmallows. In a saucepan, heat Crisco, margarine, cocoa, and RC Cola. Bring mixture to a boil, then pour it over the flour, sugar, and marshmallows. Stir in buttermilk, baking soda, and eggs. Pour into in a greased tube pan and bake at 350°F for 45 minutes.

Or substitute white cake mix, lemon zest, and Mello Yello for a lemon-flavored cake.

MR. PIBB TURKEY

To create a lovely golden brown turkey, pour a can of Mr. Pibb over the bird before you put it in the oven. The sugar will crystallize on the turkey's skin, and the meat will have a slightly fruity flavor.

CHERRY COKE SALAD

1 box black cherry Jell-O
1 can drained, crushed pineapple
1 can black bing cherries
1/2 cup pecans
1 envelope unflavored gelatin
1 can Cherry Coke

Heat juice from the cherries. Add the other ingredients, leaving the Coke for last. Pour into a mold and chill until solid.

DR PEPPER PUNCH

For a quick boost, heat a mugful of Dr Pepper in the microwave, then throw in a teaspoon of instant coffee and a lemon slice. It's a great way to mainline sugar and caffeine.

GOURMET DISHES

This section is indispensable for frugal foodies who love to surprise and delight their friends.

CANNED MUSHROOM CAVIAR

1 small unpeeled eggplant, chopped
1 medium onion, chopped
1/4 cup chopped green pepper
4 ozs. canned mushrooms, drained and chopped
2 cloves garlic, chopped
1/3 cup oil
1/2 cup chopped black olives
1/4 cup capers, drained
1 1/4 cups water
6 ozs. tomato paste

2 tbsp. wine vinegar
½ tsp. oregano
1½ tsp. sugar
Salt and pepper to taste

Combine eggplant, onion, green pepper, mushrooms, garlic, and oil in a pan. Cover and simmer for 10 minutes. Stir, then add the remaining ingredients. Cover and simmer for 25 minutes. Chill or store in freezer. Serve on melba toast.

PÂTÉ DE VEAU AU CHÂTEAU BLANC (WHITE CASTLE PÂTÉ)

In upstate New York, a bunch of Burger King employees used frozen burgers to skate around the kitchen before putting them on the broiler. It was all fun and floor hockey until they got caught and were charged with food tampering. (Go to p. 190.)

15 White Castle regular hamburgers
Water
2 cloves garlic
½ tsp. onion salt
Butter-flavored Crisco
1 pkg. whipped cream cheese
Sliced Spanish olives

In a blender, pulverize hamburgers (with buns), adding water as necessary. Add garlic and onion salt. Blend more.

Grease a 9 × 5-inch loaf pan with Crisco. Scrape hamburger mixture into the pan, and press smooth. Bake at 325°F for 45 minutes. Turn onto plate. Cool. Frost with cream cheese. Garnish with olives, and serve with toast points.

TWINKIE TIRAMISÚ

"Take some instant coffee crystals, Kahlúa, and Hershey's syrup. Find a Hostess Twinkie and mush them all together for a lovely post-meal tiramisú. If none of these supplies are available who cares? Dessert is always incidental."

—Stuart M. Teigen, Twinkie fan

STYLISH TV DINNER

And if that doesn't chip your beef, take a spork to your TV dinner. De-tray it, add a few garnishes, and you've got gourmet! See for yourself: *Garnishes:* lemon, parsley, mini marshmallows, Spanish olives, sliced red pepper.

BEFORE   AFTER

KITCHEN COSMETICS

"You'd be surprised how much it costs to look this cheap."

—Dolly Parton

You don't have to spend Dolly's millions to look good, and Dolly didn't either—before she hit the Grand Ol' Opry that is. The Parton girls, born into a long line of sharecroppers in the Smoky Mountains, used Mercurochrome (remember that red crap they put on your knees when you fell on the playground?) to redden their lips and the blackened ends of burnt matches for eyeliner. During those tough times, Dolly also used vinegar to soothe a sunburn and flour to powder her nose. Sometimes she put on so much flour her mother warned she'd be "sweating biscuits" at school.

BAKING BEAUTY

"Just because it's food, doesn't mean you can't put it on your face."

—Demorge Brown, Port Arthur, Texas

Coffee Cellulite Shrinker: In the shower, rub coffee grinds on flabby thighs to reduce the appearance of cellulite. Fergie and Cindy Crawford both swear by it. Caffeine is the main ingredient in all those expensive "cellulite reduction" creams. Caffeine is a diuretic, which dehydrates the tissues, making them shrink, and helps to draw out toxins. It's also a vasoconstrictor, which firms up the skin. For extra smoothing, "celebrity beauty coach" Diane Irons suggests you rub your

thighs with coffee grinds and then wrap them tightly in Saran Wrap for a few minutes. To smooth the dimples out further, roll the Saran-Wrapped thighs with a rolling pin.

Egg-White Face Pack: The protein in egg whites feeds your skin, and the elastic properties of the whites tightens your pores as it dries. To make a face pack, take two egg whites and a pinch of cornstarch. Whip it all up, then smear the mixture on your face. Leave it on for two minutes, then rinse it off with water. Deborah Rutledge, beauty specialist, says that raw egg white is the best thing you could possibly put on your face. Her seventy-two-year-old mother has used it all her life and hardly looks a day over forty.

Hen Fruit Shampoo: "Hen fruit" is trucker-speak for "eggs," and if you want to be truly gorgeous, you'll need a lot of them. The protein in eggs nourishes hair follicles and repairs damaged ends . . .

1 egg
½ tsp. vegetable oil
½ tsp. lemon juice (blondes only)
1 cup commercial shampoo

Whisk the ingredients together for a gentle, conditioning shampoo.

"People need to know about natural remedies that are cheaper than something at the Lancome counter."—Diane Irons

Bananas for Limp, Lifeless Hair: Mash up a banana along with a quarter cup of honey and a quarter cup molasses. Massage the mixture into clean, damp hair. Leave it there for twenty minutes, then wash and condition your hair as usual. The banana moisturizes, the honey will make your thatch shine like chrome, and the molasses adds body. The Body Shop swears by these ingredients, so why shouldn't you?

Orange Juice Curlers: Forget curlers . . . use frozen orange juice cans to make your big puffy curls. Roll cans into wet hair. Blow dry. Hair spray. (Remember to remove cans.)

Tips for Zits

TOMATO RUB: Blackheads? Rub a tomato slice on your nose. It's an exfoliant, and the acidity kills zit-producing bacteria.

(DON'T) COAT YOUR FACE WITH TOOTHPASTE: Toothpaste helps dry up pimples. It contains both calcium carbonate and floride salts, which drive away moisture and oils. But because it can be harsh, just dab the paste on your zits, not anywhere else.

BUTTERMILK works as a nondrying astringent.

SPA

Kitty Litter Face Pack: Diane Irons, "celebrity beauty coach," discovered that many of the incredibly expensive spas doing masks were using mud and not fancy mud either. They were using Kitty Litter made of 100 percent dried clay. Here's how: Mix a tablespoon of the clay litter with a little water to make a paste and then slap it on your face. Wait for it to dry, then rinse it off with water. Do it—Christy Brinkley does.

Kool-Aid Hair Dye: Want to be a redhead? Try dyeing your hair with cherry Kool-Aid. Mix a packet of unsweetened Kool-Aid with a little water. Using rubber gloves to keep your hands clean, rub the Kool-Aid paste through your hair. Let dry for half an hour. Wash hair. (FYI: Toothpaste can be used to remove stains left on the skin after dying. Dab the toothpaste on the stain and rub it away. Rinse.)

Tennis Academy Sunscreen: In *Infinite Jest*, David Foster Wallace's characters layer themselves with Lemon Pledge to create an impermeable, waterproof sunscreen before a match. But the logic is probably "what works for wood works for me" which is probably not very good logic. The characters also say the Pledge starts to smell like skunk when they sweat.

Dried Bean Foot Massage: For a relaxing foot massage, Heloise, the Household Hints Lady, suggests that you put dried beans in your sneakers and walk slowly around the house.

The key to completing the at-home beauty spa is giving yourself a manicure and pedicure. To make your polish job last longer, rub horse hoof lacquer (e.g., Hooflex) on your nails. Broken nail? Cut out a little piece of gauze from a dry, unused tea bag. Put it over the crack in your fingernail and put nail polish over it.

LEMON JUICE

The citric acid in lemon juice is a bleaching agent, and every asshole knows you can put lemon juice in your hair to make it blond, but here are some things you might not have heard of:

- **Exfoliating Lemonade**: Squeeze the juice out of half a lemon, then stir in a teaspoon of sugar. Put some of this stuff in the palm of your hand and add a little soap lather. Scrub your face and you'll feel the difference.
- **Lemon Freckle Buster**: Mix two ounces of fresh squeezed lemon juice with a teaspoon of glycerine. Shake it up in a little bottle and apply to freckles with a cotton ball. The lemon juice, of course, is a bleaching agent, and the glycerine will hold moisture in the outer layer of the skin, thus ensuring that the freckles are treated to the lemon's full capacity.

MAYONNAISE

It can save a sandwich or a salad, but it can be used liberally on many other things. The oil will soak into anything.

- **Mayo Conditioner**: Massage mayonnaise into your hair. Wrap your head (not your face) with Saran Wrap and cover with a towel. Let sit for thirty minutes, then wash your hair.
- **Mayo Moisturizer**: Gently massage full-fat mayonnaise into your face, to soothe dry skin.
- **Miracle Whip** soothes sunburns.

"April's hair, however, hung down like cooked spinach."
—Norman Mailer, *The Executioner's Song*

Ketchup Color Cure: If your blond locks turn green from too much swimming pool, massage ketchup into your hair and let it sit for thirty minutes. Then wash it out. You may have to do this a few times for the full effect, but the end result is truly spinach free.

Slimming Down?: Drink a glass of vinegar before each meal. Apple cider vinegar is best because it is gentlest on your stomach. The skeletal Joan Crawford did this for years—and clearly it worked. For additional weight loss, put canned meats, soups, etc., in the fridge. Fat will rise to the top of the can so you can scrape it off. A word to the wise: Do not bother doing this with SPAM. Even the low-fat version is so loaded with fat, there's no way you'll be able to get it all off. And if you did, it wouldn't be SPAM anymore—even "low-fat" SPAM is pushing SPAM somewhere it doesn't want to be.

Bubble Bath: Mix 2 cups of vegetable oil, 3 tablespoons of shampoo, and ¼ teaspoon of perfume. Throw it in the blender for a minute or so.

Removing Eye Makeup: After a night at the track, do your man a favor and use canola oil. Face it: No one likes to wake up next to a raccoon.

Dry Shampoo: Cornstarch absorbs moisture and can be used in place of regular body or foot powder after a refreshing shower. And if you don't have time to shower, consider a dry shampoo: Sprinkle cornstarch in your hair and rub it around. It will absorb some of the grease and make you look less skanky. (Baby powder works too.)

Crisco Belly: When pregnant, rubbing Crisco on your belly should keep the skin lubricated and flexible, thus reducing the appearance of stretch marks.

Turkey Baster + Yogurt = Relief: Ladies, to cure a yeast infection fill a turkey baster with plain yogurt, slip it into your glory hole, and squirt. Remove the now-empty baster (make sure to clean it before next Thanksgiving), and lie down for a while to let the acidophilus do its business. Drinking cranberry juice can also eliminate a urinary tract infection because it acidifies your urine enough to kill the *E. coli* bacteria causing the infection.

Out of Aquafresh?: Cowboys used to brush their teeth with sand, but before you revert to that, baking soda mixed with salt and a few

---

Tips for Tits

Banana Bra: Zsa Zsa Gabor packs an old bra with mashed bananas and wears it around the house to keep firm. And Marilyn Monroe slept in a bra every night, trying to keep her tits up.

Wet T-shirt Tips: Prepping tits for wet T-shirt competition? Two-time champion Babs J. Stevens, of Des Moines, Iowa, believes that it's best to get out there when you're really PMSing because your boobs are at their "biggest" and "bounciest." And Babs recommends that you rub your nipples with ice for extra perk just before the douse-down.

We Must Increase Our Bust: Exercises to make your bust bigger actually just make the muscles underneath bigger. But that can still help fill out a shirt.

Do-It-Yourself Wonder Bra: For killer cleavage, stick boobs together with duct tape.

---

drops of water makes an effective toothpaste. For extra whitening, try using hydrogen peroxide instead of water.

Parsley Breath Freshener: Chlorophyll neutralizes the odoriferous bacteria in your body and really is awesome for stinkers. You can get a concentrated dose of chlorophyll from parsley. Eat a bunch of parsley, and it will not only freshen your breath, it will also help minimize BO and smelly feet too.

BOOZE

- **Alcohol** kills germs and works as an astringent. **Wine** can also help treat a pizza face. Simply soak a cotton ball in Thunderbird, and dab your blemishes with it. To maintain a clear complexion, bathe your whole face in wine daily. White is recommended for fair skins and red for darker.
- **Vodka Aftershave:** This stuff is only for tough guys. It stings like hell, but it does the job. Mix together:
  1/4 cup vodka
  1/4 cup water
  1/4 cup glycerin
  1/4 cup witch hazel

ELIMINATE WRINKLES

"The five most stolen items in drugstores are batteries, cosmetics, film, sunglasses, and, get this, Preparation H," claims Vince Staten in his article "Do Pharmacists Sell Farms?" People are too embarrassed to buy Preparation H, but its main ingredient, shark liver oil, does more than shrink hemorrhoids. It will shrink any tissue—it's a vasoconstrictor—a secret that many older women in Florida and Conan O'Brian share. And they swear by the tube that it reduces wrinkles.

- For a really lustrous shine, rinse your hair in **beer** (any kind will do).
- To remove shampoo buildup, rinse your hair in **vodka**. Or do like Jamie Lee Curtis and use **mouthwash** instead.
- You can make **hair spray** out of unflavored gelatin, **vodka**, and pure water . . . You can also mix Elmer's glue and water together to make your hair stand on end, but it won't ever want to come back down.

Speaking of hair spray, Mary Ellen Pinkham of Home and Garden Television claims that aerosol hair spray is a great way to control pests: "Spray an annoying flying bug with hair spray and its wings will stiffen, causing it to fall to the ground." Yeah, sure lady.

BIG HAIR

"I dread havin' to wash it—I'll probably have to use the Formula 21 to get it out."—Big Hair Contestant, First Annual Redneck Games

Big hair is big status for the ladies. Sadly, the Big Hair Contest has been eliminated from the Redneck Games. No one knows exactly why, but an insider suggested that perhaps it was because in 1996 a man sporting an impressive pair of Daisy Dukes and calling himself Alice ended up stealing the show. Al Szekely won after emptying an entire can of hair spray onto his head and garnishing his 'do with mini American flags. He was said to be concealing several beers in his curls.

SEX AND SODA

While we're not necessarily going to go into the whole whipped cream scene, it is important to note that one of the great free democratic pastimes is sex, and ingenuity doesn't exclude the use of food.

You've always got zucchini, green banana, and cucumber dildos. Saran Wrap condoms. Egg white lubricants. And even if Clinton didn't have time to try Altoids-enhanced oral sex at the mouth of Ms. Lewinsky, the peppermint blow job's been around long before fancy-ass British mints in a tin showed up. Doesn't anybody remember "Double your pleasure, double your fun . . . ?"

Of course, teenagers will say anything and believe everything that gets them a step closer to getting laid. Two totally false but worthy favorites:

Mountain Dew Is a Male Contraceptive: For at least ten years it has been running through the rumor mill that men can drastically reduce their sperm count by drinking Mountain Dew. Impotency for some, birth control for others. Why do people believe this? Some say it's the Yellow #5, while others claim it's the extra-large caffeine kick the Dew gives you. (Actually sperm, like their daddy, are more alert and effective on caffeine than off.) Jonathon Harris, a public affairs manager for PepsiCo, likened this contraception myth to stories about seeing Elvis at the convenience store as not simply untrue but "absurd, unfounded, and ridiculous."

Coca-Cola Is a Spermacide: In the '50s and '60s some believed that using a Coke or Dr Pepper douche after sex would prevent pregnancy.

Idiot Box

According to the *Herald Sun* in Durham, North Carolina, a horrified ninth-grade science teacher overheard this at school:

GIRL 1: I won't get pregnant tonight. I'll drink a Mountain Dew, which will kill most of the sperm cells.

GIRL 2: Shouldn't your *boyfriend* drink the Mountain Dew?

GIRL 1: He only likes Pepsi.

Not true, but the sugar and acid in the soda kills sperm, the six-ounce bottle was the perfect application size, and if you gave the bottle a good shake, the carbonation would shoot the soda all the way in. The spermicidal qualities of Coke were even tested during the public fury over "New Coke" in the '80s at the Harvard Medical school. But while Dr. Sharee Umpierre did find that Coke does kill sperm trapped in a petri dish, all it will do inside a girl is help her grow a yeast infection.

APHRODISIACS

Chocolate: Giving chocolate to your lover on Valentine's Day is more than just a token gesture—it actually contains an endorphin called phenylethylamine (PEA), which is normally excreted into the bloodstream when you are around someone you are attracted to and turns you on. *Note:* In spite of this, green M&Ms do *not* turn you into a raging horn dog, although Lord knows, people have tried.

Drano Gender Test

Some people believe that if a pregnant woman pisses on Drano crystals, the resulting color will determine the gender of her baby. Not only is it purest horseshit, you might even singe your minge. All of the following variations have been sworn by as "the key" to interpreting the Drano test:

1. Bluish yellow = boy   Greenish brown = girl

2. Brownish = boy   No change = girl

3. Brown = boy   Green = girl

4. Black = boy   Blue = girl

5. Blue = boy   Green = girl

BUT LET'S TELL THE TRUTH:
1. Blue = too much lite beer
2. Green = you're dehydrated
3. Brown = you're on the rag

Drano is also, with equal amounts of horseshit, considered a pregnancy test. The theory is, if it doesn't change color, you're not pregnant. If it does change color, you are.

Sowing Your Oats: Oats contain avena sativa, which is sold as a health food supplement to revive a flagging libido.

Celery Root: Encourages blood flow to the pelvic region.

Bananas and Oysters: Also considered to be aphrodisiacs, although it's not because of what's in them. It's because of the body parts they remind us of . . .

Jell-O Wrestling: And last but not least, the world of sport food. What's *your* favorite flavor? It takes 2,300 boxes of Jell-O to fill an 8-foot-square padded box to about 2 inches deep. Red and green are the preferred colors, because they show up best. And there is no sugar in wrestling Jell-O, because it gets too sticky.

Kraft Foods Inc. has become increasingly upset with the sexy associations building up around its oh-so-family product. But, then again, they also oppose the "Jell-O Jump," which is all about kids sliding down a chute into a big vat of their dessert.

Cars

In the cracker community, rigs rule. There are two classes of people: High class are those who have at least one vehicle that runs, and no class refers to everyone else. And not every car can be a cracker car. A suitable vehicle must be a classic American truck or an American-made steel-bodied passenger sedan. And most important, these vehicles must be able to be "worked on." "Working on" sharpens the mind, quickens the blood, and breeds all kinds of ingenuity. Of course, "working on" not only refers to keeping the thing running, it also refers to the source of much civic pride and backyard expertise: customizing.

MODS FOR THE AGES

"Is your truck tough?"—Traditional greeting

FORD TOUGH

Cracker ingenuity and the car have a long strong history together. When automaker Henry Ford released the first assembly-line car—the Model-T—cars were for the first time available on a working man's budget. Their popularity exploded, and Ford sold 15 million of them by the time he discontinued the model in 1928. To keep production prices down, Ford exercised a little ingenuity of his own. He sent investigators out to junkyards, not to find out what went wrong with his cars, but to find out which parts never failed. Then he had those parts made more cheaply. Ford also ordered that the parts coming in from subcontractors be delivered in wooden crates of a specific size, so the wood from the crate itself could be used as floorboards for the T. Even after the T retired, the Ford remained a longtime favorite with people who depended on their cars.

Detroit, Michigan

Dear Sir:
 While I still have got breath in my lungs I will tell you what a dandy car you make. I have drove Fords exclusively when I could get away with one. For sustained speed and freedom from trouble the

Ford has got every other car skinned, and even if my business hasent been strickly legal it don't hurt anything to tell you what a fine car you got in the V8.

Yours truly
Clyde Champion Barrow
(written April 10, 1934)

Of course, those cars wouldn't be where they are today if not for the modifications made by the few, the proud, the bootleggers . . .

MOONSHINER MODS

In the thirties and forties, there came to be an infamous game of cat and mouse between the bootleggers and the authorities. Some, like Tim Flock, race car driver and whiskey tripper, felt it was friendly competition: "The sheriffs were proud of us, really, but they had to catch us to exist themselves . . ." But others, like Curtis "Pops" Turner, who made his first run at ten years old, felt it was not so friendly. "Don't believe any of this stuff about how it was a game and all, and how everybody was real nice to everybody. They was playin' for keeps and shootin' real bullets." (Go to p. 190.)

Either way, the stakes got higher, and the odds were always in favor of the fastest car. According to Flock, "The city of Atlanta put a bulletin out to all the sheriff's departments that if you caught one of these bootleg cars, on Saturday morning they'd put it at auction in front of the courthouse, and the po-lice officer or the sheriff who caught the car got half the money. So man, they went crazy. They wasn't making no money anyway, and when one of these things was auctioned off, they might make a hundred bucks apiece . . . It got so bad guys would starve to death that was hauling the liquor. So we'd come up with every kind of gimmick. We done everything in the world to these cars to try and get that 90 or 120 gallons of liquor back."

And this is how the mods began. The sheriffs would figure a way to catch the moonshiners, and the moonshiners would figure out how to get away. Sometimes the game went like this:

ROUND 1
- **Bootlegger's Tip-off Mod:** Rip out back seats to make room for the booze.
- **Authorities' Response:** Spot a seatless car heading up into the woods. Wait for it to come back out. Shoot a hole in the radiator as it passes. Wait for the water to leak out. An hour later, drive up the road a mile or two to find the car out of water, overheated, stalled out, and abandoned. You win, easy.

ROUND 2
- **Bootlegger's Radiator Mod:** Put the radiator in the trunk and run hoses up through the car to the engine. Then put a half-inch metal plate in front where the radiator used to be. The sheriffs shoot the metal plate instead of the radiator. They wait in the woods and you go on your merry way.

- **Authorities' Response:** Install a "cowcatcher" on the front of your car. A cowcatcher is like a large pair of tongs. Run up on a loaded whiskey car as it labors up a hill, and clamp the tongs down on the bootlegger's rear fender. Ride the brake until you drag the whiskey car to a stop. Bootleggers run; you win their car.

ROUND 3
- **Bootlegger's Funny Fender Mod:** Attach the fender to the car with two coat hangers instead of bolts. Cowcatcher clamps; the whole fender falls off and gets tangled in the sheriff's wheels. They get stuck, you go on your merry way.
- **Authorities' Response:** Get aggressive like Jim Malt of the China Grove ATF, and put a double fender on your car in front and try to ram the bootleggers off the side of a mountain. But remember: You may win, but you lose your gaming partner *and* you lose their car.

ROUND 4
- **Bootlegger's Bomb:** Throw a gallon of whiskey through the windshield of the chasing car. It usually works, but you have one less gallon of whiskey to sell.

PLAN B
- **The Numbers Game:** Do like Pops Turner's dad: "He'd buy a whole boxcar load of Oldsmobiles—unload 'em right at the railroad siding—convert 'em and run 'em in caravan five or six at a time. He figured somebody'd always get through" (Pops Turner).

In the end, the bootleggers found their greatest advantage was to drive better and drive a faster car.

Al's Bulletproof Caddy

Al Capone wasn't exactly the kind of guy you'd find driving through the West Virginia woods, but he was a bootlegger all the same, and he had a bootlegger's kind of car: He bought a 1928 Cadillac Series 341—the same kind the police were using—and had it painted black and green—the same colors the police cruisers were painted. But it was more than just a look-alike car: Capone had his bulletproofed by adding a quarter-inch boiler plate panel all around and under the soft top, and installing inch-thick windows. He also had the rear window mounted on hinges so it could be dropped back into the car and he could shoot pursuers.

Getaway Mods: Whiskey haulers would put heavy-duty springs and cross springs in their cars, add extra shocks and carburetors, install hydraulic brakes, swap out transmissions, rebuild engines, change the rear gears and anything else to get an edge. Some claimed they could jigger their cars to get them going 160 mph uphill, fully loaded.

Pick Your Mechanic: Back in the day, there were shops that never touched anything but whiskey cars. These mechanics knew how to use mods to get cars to accelerate to top speed as quickly as possible and to muscle up hills without losing long-range staying power. The mechanics were good, but, then again, with a garage bill of $3,000 on a wanted car, they'd damn well better be.

Pick Your Car: The '34-'35 and '38 Fords were choice among whiskey trippers, but according to bootlegger Jack Smith, the '36 Ford "was a bad one because the way the steering geometry and all was."

"Setup" Cars: A setup car was a car the bootleggers used in the city to deliver small amounts of liquor to "retail" bootleggers who sold it by the pint or the glass. The key to these cars was not to have them run fast uphill like the long-range cross-country whiskey cars, but to have a quick start, so they could outrun the cops from block to block. The bootleggers built special transmissions in these cars to give them a quick speed burst. These transmissions and other setup car mods were later used in dragsters.

"You fixed a car where it would jump from block to block just as fast as it would run in twenty blocks because that was the i-dee, to outrun that man two or three blocks. They didn't have no radios back at that time. They didn't have no picture machines—no radar—and your object was to get away . . . If you could run and hide from him and unload it, there wasn't nothing he could do." (Jack Smith)

Moonshine Motor Fuel

NASCAR racers use alcohol-fueled engines, and there have been movements in the cracker outsider community since the seventies to promote moonshine fuel and "gasohol," which is a mixture of alcohol and gas that can be used in any unmodified gas engine. The rally for combustible white lightning got the ATF to relax its rules against the moonshine production business, and nowadays it is actually legal to make a liquor still at home if you can prove you're going to use it to make fuel and get a permit from the feds.

"BE A BETTER DRIVER"

Legend: Pops Turner, who won 357 races before he was through, once explained the "bootlegger's turn"—a way to spin a speeding whiskey car around 180 degrees in its own tracks in order to switch directions really fast—to a California journalist. The journalist didn't believe him, so Pops demonstrated one for him in the middle of a Los Angeles freeway. An irate state trooper quickly pulled Turner off the freeway for going the wrong direction. But when Turner explained that he was going the wrong direction on account of the bootlegger's turn, and once again explained the turn to the trooper, the disbelieving trooper offered to let him go if he could do the turn again . . . which he did.

Fact: Pete Waldmeir of the *Detroit News* reported a North Carolina state trooper found Turner's car upside down in a ditch, with Pops suspended helplessly by the seat belt. The trooper smelled booze in the car and asked, "Say, mister, you drunk?" Pops replied, "Of course. What the hell do you think I am, a stunt driver?"

EARLY STOCK CAR RACING

"In the early days, they'd just as soon fight as drive. They'd even stop the race and fight." —Junior Johnson

The desire to find better cars and better drivers among moonshiner moguls led to a challenge for them to put the money where their motor was, and a race to find out who had the fastest car was staged in the cow pastures of Stockbridge, Georgia, in 1934. Soon these races took place every Sunday, and hundreds of spectators would come out to lay bets and watch the races. So it was, out there in the grass pastures, that stock car racing was born. Open-wheel racing had been around for years, but the cars were expensive and it wasn't until the moonshiners started racing their mods that anybody could do it.

From there, stock car racing quickly organized a rough and rowdy circuit using tracks built out of dirt, sand, and cracker ingenuity.

The first stock car races were called "early model races" and had no modification restrictions on the cars. People fixed up old cars, belted themselves in with a piece of rope, strapped the doors shut with chains or leather straps, and were ready to race. In the early races, a major problem was blowing out tires. The tire companies hadn't yet developed vulcanized rubber to withstand extreme pressure, so when the tires got hot on the track, the air inside them would expand (from 40 pounds of

> "Dirt track racing, I think, was more fun . . . Racing was more fun back then than it is today, and the further back you go, the more fun it was." —JACK SMITH

pressure to 60 pounds) and the tires would pop. Clever racers figured out they could fill the tires with nitrogen instead of air, because the nitrogen wouldn't expand in the heat and cause the tires to pop.

But by the time "late model racing," known as the Grand Nationals, was created, the promoters were very strict on the mods allowed. The cars had to come with standard factory equipment, which was the beginning of the end of cracker ingenuity at the track. These kinds of "stock" car racing rules still govern NASCAR today.

Cracker Tracks: In an attempt to compete with the brick-paved Indianapolis Bowl track—which was for fancy open-wheel cars only—Big Bill France, the founder of NASCAR, opened his own track for stock cars in Daytona in February 1948. And he did it without the benefit of bricks: The course France promoted was a two-mile stretch of Florida Highway A1A connected to a two-mile stretch of beach by two U-turns.

Another promoter, Harold Brasington, built a track named Darlington in 1950 on land donated by farmer Sherman Ramsey in return for shares in the raceway corporation. The land contained both a fish pond and a minnow pond. Ramsey said the fish pond could go, but the minnow pond had to stay. Because of that pond, Darlington came out shaped like a pear instead of the traditional oval. Barney Wallace, a peanut broker and another one of the investors, explained, "We built the track the way we did because that's the way it came out."

The 1950 racing season opened on the beach at Daytona in February and closed at Darlington on Labor Day, with hundreds of races in between on dirt tracks all across the Piedmont Plateau. The

Plateau, which runs from Richmond, Virginia, to South Georgia, has ideal soil for homemade dirt tracks. Half- and quarter-mile dirt tracks sprang up everywhere, and anyone with a rig could give it a go.

CUSTOMIZED

After World War II, GIs came back looking to buy new cars. But because of the war effort, only old cars and cars made from old molds were available, so these young men started customizing old cars themselves to give them a modern look. The idea behind customizing was to make the body look long, sleek, and low. Customizers would remove all the chrome trim from the car, fill in seams, chop the tops, and channel and lower the bottoms. To make the cars really slick, some would add special wheels, sink antennas and lights into the body of the coach, and remove door handles, bumpers, and even the radiator grill.

Customized cars had to be driven carefully to keep from hitting the ground if they were too low and too heavy from all the lead filler used in customizing. These cars became known as "lead sleds" or "low-and-slows."

ROD RAGE

For those who weren't interested in low-and-slows, another kind of rod had been coming into its own since the thirties. *Hot rods* ("rod" is short for "roadster," and "hot" means "modified," not stolen) were also customs, but the key difference between a hot rod and a lead sled, or "street rod," was that hot rods were built to "perform" rather than "cruise." Hot rods were equipped with high-performance V-8 engines and heavy-duty shocks. By the fifties, these cars were sometimes known as street machines and used for street racing, games of chicken, and speed, speed, speed.

Rod Mod Lingo

BOBBED: When fenders, etc., are shortened or cut down in length. Veteran bobber Bill W. says the term originated in the 1950s, when girls cut their hair short and called it "bobbed."

CHANNELED: When the floor is raised to allow for a car body to be lowered so that from the outside, the body sits closer to the ground, but there is still room for the chassis underneath.

CHOPPED: When equal sections of the posts supporting a closed car roof are cut out in order to lower the entire roof.

FLAMES: Painted flames became a popular motif on hot rods to signify they were built for speed.

FRENCHED: When antennas, license plates, lights, sidelights, door handles, etc., are recessed into the body of the car.

FUZZY DICE: Hung from the rearview mirror of a hot rod, the dice were symbolic of the way in which a hot-rodder spent his life "dicing with death."

HOPPED: When a high-performance engine is put into an older car.

LOWERED: After it is channeled, the entire body of the car is lowered over the wheels so it is closer to the ground.

PHANTOM: A rod that is so extensively modified with parts from different cars that it no longer has any resemblance to any single model car.

RAKED: When a car is lowered in front only.

HOT-ROD MUSCLE CARS

Muscle cars borrow from both the "lead sled" and the "hot rod." First appearing in the 1950s, they adopted the drag race look but went high instead of low, using huge wheels and tires on the rear and skinny ones at the front. And if you didn't already have a seriously big motor in your car, you needed to at least make it look like you did. More trademarks of the "hot-rod muscle" style are:

- the side exhaust pipe just in front of the rear wheel,
- the spoiler on the trunk, and
- the air dam under the front and the scoop on the hood.

KUSTOM KINGS

George Barris started making "kustom" cars for Hollywood film and TV in the early 1950s. The age of the hot rod was in full force, but George Barris and his brother Sam took it up a notch, dominating the screen with their dazzling cars. They made cars for films like *Hot Rod Rumble, Cool Hot Rod, Hot Rod Girl*, and, of course, *Rebel Without a Cause.*

By the 1960s, hot rods were out, but Barris was still in, making custom cars for movie and music stars, including John Wayne, Elvis Presley, Frank Sinatra, Dean Martin, The Beach Boys, Jerry Lewis, Sonny & Cher, Steve McQueen, and more. He also built the wild one-of-a-kind cars in the TV shows *The Munsters, The Green Hornet, My Mother the Car, Mannix*, and *The Beverly Hillbillies*. But his most famous car is the Batmobile from the sixties TV show *Batman and Robin.*

Barris was the last owner of his friend James Dean's infamous death car, a Porsche Spyder with a deadly bite.

Dicing with Death Jimmy Dean, Jimmy Dean

JIMMY: Why do we do this?
BUZZ: You have to do something.
—JAMES DEAN to his nemesis in *Rebel Without a Cause*

In 1955 Dean bought a silver Porsche Spyder, planning to race it in Salinas. Barris painted racing stripes and the insignia "little bastard" on the side of the car, but only hours later, Dean was killed when he crashed on the way to the races.

Barris bought the wreck to use for parts, and trouble continued . . . While unloading the Spyder at Barris's garage, it fell off the delivery truck and broke his mechanic's leg. Two doctors bought the engine and drive train, respectively, to put in their own race cars. On October 2, 1956, they both raced their cars using the parts for the first time. During the race, one was killed in one accident, and the other was seriously injured in another.

Barris used the wrecked Spyder body as part of a driving safety exhibit for high school kids. While on tour, a warehouse housing Dean's car burned down, but the car survived. It broke into pieces during one show, and was later involved in several other fatal accidents. Finally, in 1960, the car was shipped from Miami back to Los Angeles . . . But somewhere along the way it vanished.

"They finished with a show, they put (the Spyder) on a truck. The truck comes out here. Eight days later, we open the truck, there's no car. Gone . . . Even today when I do shows, people pull me aside and say, 'I know where it is.' They say it's in a garage or in the ground or up in a hayloft, or put away inside a truck. I don't care where I go—the littlest town or the biggest town—I'll always have somebody come up and say they know where that car is hidden . . . But we never to this day found the car."

—George Barris, as quoted in the *L.A. Times*, 1989

CAR ART AND ART CARS

In southern California, Ed "Big Daddy" Roth joined the postwar custom craze, modifying old cars. But by the late 1950s, he was building his cars completely from scratch. He used junkyard parts and fiberglass (which was new at the time) to build his first Kustom Kar, named "Outlaw," which was as much sculpture as car. Roth soon became known as "Big Daddy" and was an inspiration to artists and do-it-yourselfers all over the country.

"There is one art show that rolls through Houston in the spring that even New York and San Francisco can't match."
—*AUTOWEEK*, 1996

In the early sixties, while working on other cars, Big Daddy became famous for his cartoons of a hot-rod-driving monster named Rat Fink and his friends, Mother's Worry, Drag Nut, and Mr. Gasser. These monsters captured the teenage imagination. They appeared on T-shirts and album covers all over the country, and suddenly everyone wanted Big Daddy's creations. To

A beaded car, on display at the Art Car Parade.

David Best's car "Faith" has the blinkers in the nostrils of the buffalo mounted on the hood.

meet the demand, Roth expanded his garage, and with dozens helping him make T-shirts, album covers, and Kustom Kars, some called it the blue-collar version of Andy Warhol's Factory. Big Daddy Roth died April 4, 2001, but he will always be a Kustom inspiration, and the "Big Daddy" of art cars.

Art cars take customizing to its most colorful end. The cars must be street legal, but otherwise there are no limits to what people can do. In the early 1980s a guy named Gene Pool (his real name) covered his car with sticky adhesives and sprinkled grass seeds on them. He drove around, the grass grew, and Gene had a "Grass Car."

For over a decade, the Art Car Parade has been held every spring in Houston and is sponsored by the Orange Show, another haven of cracker ingenuity (see page 38). Each year, the parade draws up to two hundred and fifty of the best art cars around. A shark-shaped car, a two-story hearse covered in skulls, a red high-heeled shoe built over a motorcycle frame that goes forty miles an hour and has room for two ... these cars kick.

If you use a motorcycle engine, art cars are still street legal without a windshield or seatbelts. This one was made from a combination of a motorcycle and lawnmower parts.

AWESOME MODS

WOODIES

Back in the sixties, California surfers loved wood-bodied station wagons, known as "woodies," which were perfect for stashing surf equipment. Surfers would fix their woodies up with shag carpeting and sleeping bags so that they could sleep, ride, and travel from beach to beach without having to stop at a motel.

MOBILE CAR POOL

The "Car Pool" is The World's Only Fully Functional Driving Hot Tub, put together by a bunch of clever Canucks in need of a little relaxing entertainment. It all started with a 1982 Chevrolet Malibu:

"The first version had a rubber liner to contain the water while the driver sat on a milk crate and pushed the pedals through the liner. Since then, the Car Pool has improved significantly. It currently operates as follows: A Jacuzzi pool pump draws water in from the fiberglass tub through a spa cartridge filter up to the engine bay, where it enters the heat exchanger. The heat exchanger is an insulated steel box containing two heater cores. A valve in the engine bay diverts the coolant from the engine through the heater cores, where the heat is transferred to the water pumped around them. The hot water is then sent through three jets positioned to swirl and mix the water in the tub. Other notable features include the 1968 Camaro inline six-cylinder engine, a stainless steel exhaust system and the Clarion marine audio CD stereo system. It also has an DC-AC inverter so we can run the 120-volt AC pool pump off of the 12-volt DC battery when in motion."

—Andrew Hill, engineer

SPACE SHUTTLE MOD

Albert Colbert of Buena Vista, Georgia, created a "space shuttle" from a junked storage tank (rumored to be the old blood vat from the local chicken processing plant). He welded it to the frame of an old truck, installed eighteen seats inside, and gives rides around town on special occasions. When asked why he built a shuttle, Colbert explained that he'd originally wanted to do a plane (see "Hot Wings," page 13), but the wingspan was too great for the city streets.

COFFIN CARS AND SUICIDE DOORS

Suicide doors open backward: The hinges are on the back part of the door instead of the front. They got their name because if they unlatch at high speed, the wind blows them open instead of closed, allowing for passengers to tumble out into the street. The suicide door was last seen in mass production on the 1960s Lincoln Continental, the car JFK was riding in when he was shot down in Dallas. But these days, backward-opening doors are making a comeback on the custom circuit, especially on mini trucks. A side-loader is a hearse where the casket is loaded sideways through a set of suicide doors, as opposed to an end-loader, where the coffin is loaded through the tailgate. But side-loader or no, not everybody needs a hearse: In 1998 in Tiverton, Rhode Island, eighty-four-year-old Rose Martin was buried in her 1962 Corvair, which she drove for thirty-six years. Before the burial, Rose's longtime mechanic, George Murray, made some final mods on the car so the casket could fit inside: He ripped out the engine, driver's seat, and steering wheel and cut an opening in the trunk. "It was a shame to cut it up," Murray said. "But it's her car and she wanted it the way she wanted it." Rose and her Corvair were lowered to rest with a crane, taking up four burial plots.

MANUFACTURED MUSCLE

"You could sell a young man's car to an old man, but you could never sell an old man's car to a young man."—Bunkie Knudsen, manager of Pontiac in '56

(Pontiac was a trendsetter in muscle-car manufacturing)

From the 1960s until the 1973 oil crisis, muscle cars took the spirit of the street machine and put it into factory-built cars like the 409 Chevy, the Pontiac GTO, the Ford Mustang, the Chevrolet Camaro, and the Plymouth Barracuda. Bunkie Knudsen, former manager of Pontiac, was one of the champions of the muscle-car cause. First, he built a high-performance Pontiac with a hopped-up engine and twin four-barrel carburetors to compete in the Daytona speed trials in

IDIOT BOX

THE BUMPER DUMPER: Uncle Booger has given us the world's only toilet that can be bolted to the back of your car for the bargain price of $59.99. It's a toilet seat and a lid that you can screw on to your back bumper. A five-gallon bucket slides neatly beneath it to act as the bowl, so you can take a dump while you're out camping without squatting in poison ivy or having to wander around holding wads of your own dirty toilet paper. Sounds swell, but one question remains: On the way home, *where* do you put the bucket?

PEDESTRIAN PISSER: This is a simple, extremely juvenile mod. Empty the windshield-washer-fluid tank and fill it with water. Take the hose from the tank and detach it where it splits to reach the two windshield ducts. Attach another length of hose there to divert all the water. Make sure the hose is long enough so that you can reach it, and aim it at people on the street while you're driving. As you drive by, press the window-washer button, and water squirts the person instead of your window. Circling around the block and hitting the same pedestrian repeatedly is a great way to make someone really, really angry.

Florida. Then in 1957 the Bonneville (named for the Bonneville salt flats in Nevada where speed records were being set) came out with bucket seats, three carburetors, and a convertible top. To accommodate these features, the Bonneville required a wider body, so the front-end rear treads were increased by four and a half inches, which became the famous "wide track." In 1959, Knudsen compared the wide-track Pontiac to a "linebacker in ballet slippers." Next came the GTO: The world's first packaged muscle car was born and would define "muscle car" for at least a decade.

Muscle Style: Steve McQueen in *Bullitt* epitomized the life of the muscle-car driver as he engaged in high-flying car chases through the streets of San Francisco.

The General Lee of *Dukes of Hazzard* fame was a '69 Charger. The show was filmed near Gatlinburg, Tennessee, and according to a local, the stuntmen wrecked so many Chargers that they ran out. The show's producers sent scouts to supermarket parking lots to put notes under the windows of all the Chargers they could find, offering to buy the cars (and if not, at least see if the owners would be willing to have their car done up like the E. Lee and put on TV).

PICKUP TRUCKS

The long-running Ford-Chevy feud has been known to tear apart marriages, families, and trailer parks. And people get rabid about their loyalties because the truck is the staple standard of everyday transportation. Because of this, the authors of this book must remain impartial, so let's just talk about pickups, plain old pickups. These trucks aren't about chrome and fancy paint jobs; they're about getting the job done. And there's nothing that'll give a truck a life like a few

simple mods, e.g., fat off-road dirt tires, heavy-duty suspension, roll-bars, and a lift kit.

TRUCKERS

"We're not just a union; we're a Brotherhood."—Teamster

This chapter wouldn't be complete without at least a word on truck drivers. They have created their own road culture. They have their own free newspaper, called *The Trucker*, their own roadside stops, their own kind of speed, and their own truck-stop miniseries.

Elvis Presley wasn't exactly teamster material, but he was a trucker. In April 1952, he drove a truck for Crown Electric for $40 a week but kept working on his music. A month later, when Elvis auditioned for Eddie Bond's band, Bond said, "Stick to driving a truck, because you'll never make it as a singer."

LOW-RIDERS

"Low rider drives a little slower. Low rider is a real goer." —War

Low-riders are all about chopped and lowered rides, from the teeniest car to the widest truck. Riding low means getting down, way down "into the weeds." It began in the 1950s when chopped-top Fords and Mercuries were the "koolest kustoms" around. Just cut the springs in front, add lowering blocks to the rear, and hydraulic jacks . . .

The greatest form of trucker ingenuity, however, comes right out of the whiskey-tripper tradition of figuring out how to stay one step ahead of the po-lice: the CB radio. On the CB, truckers speak in code using code names (handles) because while it's not illegal to use a CB itself, most people use them to get away with speeding and doing various other illegal things on the road. They communicate with other drivers to see where the cops are and, of course, which cars house the hottest chicks, aka "seat covers." By the way, "panic in the streets" means the FCC is monitoring the airwaves.

Billy Carter's Redneck Power Pickup

Billy Carter, president Jimmy's brother, could "take care of himself," and he let everyone know it. Billy's truck, now on display in the Smoky Mountain Car Museum in Pigeon Forge, Tennessee, is called "Redneck Power" and says "Ain't Apologisin' " across the tailgate.

Trucker Code for Cops

Bear = State trooper

Mama bear = Female highway patrol officer (a regular female cop is known as a "she bear" or "city kitty")

Bear in the dark = Cop with his lights off

Bear in the grass = Cop on the median

Bear in the air = Airplane with radar unit

Feeding the bears = Paying a traffic ticket

County mounties = Sheriffs

Evel Knievel = Motorcycle cop

Plain wrapper = Unmarked police car

Charlie = FCC

Zoo = Police headquarters

Bubblegum machine = Twirling light on top of a trooper car

Advertising/blue-light special/disco lights = Descriptions of a bear on the move

Donut run = Bear driving fast but with no lights and no siren

Bird dog = Radar detector (If you have "heavy contact," the "bird dog's jumping on the dash.")

Special CB Channels

In the basement = 1

Double Harleys = 11

Baskin Robbins or "the ice cream channel" = 31

SLICK FIXES

Now let's just make it clear that not everyone dreams of driving around in a kandy-kolored GTO with fuzzy dice on the dash, mag wheels, and a bottle of Armorall. Some people are clear on the fact that a rig is for getting you where you want to go with as minimal hassle, as few mechanics, and as little money as possible. Some of the greatest ingenuity in the auto realm has been devised while "working on" cars by people who just won't let their car die.

> *"I can honestly say that, in all those years, she always brought me home, even if I had to jerry-rig the accelerator with a woman's hair barrette."*
> —Craig Jones about his truck, Lucille

Start a Car with a Screwdriver: If your ignition switch punks out and your car won't start or your key won't turn, pry the ignition barrel out of the dash and use a slot-head screwdriver to complete the circuit to start the engine.

Lockout: If you're locked out of your car and don't have a slim-jim, you can straighten out a coat hanger, bend a little hook in the end of it, and use that instead. You already know this, but what you might not know is that most lock releases are located between the lock and the edge of the door, so you should slip the slim-jim/hanger between the two. Also, not all locks are released by pulling up. Some are sideways and some are released by pushing down, so try all directions. And always try to open the passenger door.

But if the slim-jim doesn't work and it's a real emergency, you can break the lock. Jam a screwdriver into the keyhole and turn until the whole lock barrel turns. The lock will break and your car will open, but then the lock will fall out and you will have a hole in your door, if you care.

String Speed: If your accelerator cable breaks, you can always tie a string to the governor and hold it through the window. To make the car accelerate, pull the string.

Stuck?: When your number-one goal is to get traction, kitty litter, sand, branches, cardboard, or even your car mats jammed under your

tires can help get you out of a slick spot. You can also wind a rope around both powered tires for a snow-chain effect. And if you're in deep snow, a hubcap makes a decent shovel.

Leaks: Worried about what's leaking? Take the puddle color test so you know what to fix:

- Green: leaking coolant
- Red: automatic transmission fluid
- Clear/Light red: power steering
- Clear/Thick and oily: manual transmission or differential
- Blue: windshield washer
- Dark/Dirty/Black: motor oil.

Looking for the source of leaking oil? Clean and degrease engine; dry. Spray with white athletic foot powder. As the leak comes through it will stain the foot powder dark, making it easy to see.

Homemade Antifreeze: Back in the early 1900s people started pouring glycerin, honey, or calcium chloride into their radiator water as an antifreeze—and it still works.

Bake Your Battery Clean: If your battery posts are corroded, take some baking soda and water and mix it into a heavy paste, put it on the battery posts and as Josh Hancock, a technical transportation consultant, says, "Watch the corrosion go pffft! right off."

Instant Muscle: To get a car to sound like it's packing some dragster horsepower, you can remove the muffler, which is illegal and will probably get you a ticket. To get around removing the muffler, you can poke holes in it, instead. Or better yet, remove the muffler, cut a panel out of the bottom, gut the muffler, then stuff it with steel wool and seal the panel back up. Even without a V-8, you will get a throaty muscle-car rumble coming from the tailpipe.

You can also invert your intake manifold into the carburetor to make the engine sound really loud.

For more horsepower, remove the air filter, but be warned; you won't know what else gets into your engine and so you run the risk of an explosion.

Cheap Power: Use transmission fluid for your power steering. It's much cheaper, and it works. But on the other hand, do *not* put power steering fluid (which is much more expensive, anyway) into your transmission.

Chew Fuse: If you've got an old car with a blown fuse, pull it out and jam the foil wrapper from your Double-Mint gum in there instead. You'll get a connection. This is the same principal behind stuffing a penny into your fuse at home to complete the electrical circuit. Both work, but both run the risk of blowing your electrical system because there is no fuse to shut down the system if it gets overloaded.

Defeat Leaks: Some say to cure a cracked radiator block, stuff bits of steel wool into the radiator. It will melt and temporarily seal cracks. But Josh says he's never heard of this and thinks it might clog the radiator. Better to stick to the liquid sealant you can buy in a store.

A New Start: A dead starter motor can be caused by worn bristles inside the solenoid, which create a short circuit. The motor can often be temporarily revived by hitting it with a hammer.

COSMETICS

To give your car that extra something without major modifications . . .

Rust: If you live in a snowy climate and parts of your car are starting to rust through, try getting a big oil can and cutting it up. With some small nuts and bolts to hold the tin, cover your car's rust spots, then smooth it off with plastic body putty, which you should be able to get at any auto parts store.

Dents: You can hammer out dents from behind if they're on a single sheet panel, but to get at dents in tougher spots, like the doors, drill a screw into the dent, and pull on it with pliers. The dent will pop out, and when you untwist the screw, it will be a lot easier to fill the screw hole. Then Bondo the entire door.

Tires: Rub brake fluid on the tires to make them look newer. (Try used brake fluid; it's free.)

Paint: Why Microflake Is the Only Way to Go:

> *"Preferences for certain colors were closely associated with rebelliousness, and these are the very same colors many of the kids go for—purple, carnal*

yellow, various violets and lavenders and fuchsias and many other of these Kandy Kolors."—Tom Wolfe, *The Kandy-Kolored Tangerine-Flake Streamlined Baby*

What we're talking about here is body and shine. Microflakes are made of ultralight polyester and aluminum. They're very thin paints, easy to smooth out, and give your ride an awesome 3-D sparkle on top of a solid base. Apply your flakes with a spray gun, allow to dry, and then cover with a clear topcoat.

Chrome: If the chrome bumpers and strips are all pitted and rusty, take a piece of aluminum foil and rub it over the spots. A thin layer of aluminum from the foil will stick to the rust, making the chrome look almost like new.

Keep it all looking slick, 'cause you're only as hot as your ride. And that's a fact.

A spirit caddie at Paradise Gardens.

Fun

Fun doesn't have to be about sitting back in an air-conditioned movie theater, eating stale popcorn, and watching Burt Reynolds have all the shits and grins. It can be about having a good time on your own terms. Wrestling your own pig and smashing your own car, playing your own music and making your own rules. And doing it for cheap.

MOTORING

"Motorin'. . . What's your price for flight?"

—Night Ranger, "Sister Christian"

Cars aren't just for status, noise, and "working on"; they're also an easy way to get cheap thrills. In fact, ingenious cracker speed freaks have gone far beyond a traditional car race, incorporating anything that can be driven in the quest for maximum-velocity entertainment. Not that it's safe, but when things get slow, some people have a real knack for creating brilliantly destructive ways to one-up each other. Never underestimate man's ability to entertain himself with a motor and the potential for a bunch of explosions.

BACKYARD FUN

Drag Racing: Drag racing began on the streets when people raced each other from stoplight to stoplight in their hot rods. A more serious form of drag racing started in the late fifties in the Dry Lakes district of California and eventually evolved into professional track drag racing. Out on the salt flats, Don "Big Daddy" Garlits was the first drag racer to go 200 mph from a standing start in a quarter mile, then the first to hit 250 mph, and then the first to hit 270. He was most famous for inventing the rear-engine drag car after an accident in his "Swamp Rat-13" blew off half his right foot in 1970.

Chicken: Chicken is a game of nerve. Two cars race toward each other head on, and the first one to swerve loses. It's what happens when two alpha males meet. (Go to p. 62.)

Doing Donuts: If you have no friends to race against, you can get a head rush at least by doing donuts in an empty parking lot. Turn your wheel all the way to the right and start accelerating . . .

Truck Pulls: A tug of war between two trucks on a chain. Basically, all you need to do is put two trucks rear bumper to rear bumper, and attach the rear axles together with a chain. Each truck tries to pull the other. Warning: frequently fatal to transmissions.

Skitching: Skitching is all about hitching a car ride on your skateboard or roller blades. Skitchers know they have to match the speed of the car and grab onto its right side. And they know to stay as close to the side of the road as possible so they can get out of the way quickly if they fall.

Tailgate Skiing: Tailgate skiers stand up in the truck bed, holding onto a rope or a chain, and try to stay upright while the driver swerves violently, trying to knock them down.

Tailgate Parties: Drive to a designated area, flip down your tailgate, and park on it while you guzzle beer with like-minded friends. Sometimes someone will get really ambitious and turn a tailgate into a picnic table, complete with wineglasses and chairs.

IDIOT SLEDDING

Skids from the Great North: "Jason Meyer and Jeremy Johnson of Everett, Washington, made headlines last week for practicing 'idiot-sledding'—the sport of towing a ratty old chair to the dump behind a racing pickup truck with a guy in the chair. 'It's antidrug to do stuff like that,' said Johnson, to the belief of not one cop. Meyer drives a beer truck by day, to the surprise of no cop, either." —*National Post* (Canada)

If there's no snow, you can ride any drag-behind farm equipment through the dirt for a similar effect.

Bering Sea Ice Skitch: Oil-rig workers in Alaska have been known to drive out onto the frozen Bering Sea to ice-skitch: They get out of the truck and grab a chain attached to the tailgate. Holding on for dear life, they "ski" across the ice on their boots, while the driver goes faster and faster.

Ice Racing: Ice racing is where people race their cars out on frozen lakes. Any lake frozen solid enough to support a dozen cars will do, but seeing as you have little control and no brakes, it's wise to race on as large a lake as possible. Especially if you're going to get involved in a Lake Champlain teenage favorite: racing in the dark. More organized ice racers have different divisions: rubber-to-ice, studded tires, modified classes, and stock classes. But it's still all about mastering the skid. (Slip up, go to p. 62.)

BIG-TIME FUN

DIRT-TRACK RACES

Dirt-track races are a throwback to the early days of racing, before NASCAR went high tech. Dirt tracks are cut out in fields, and anyone with any kind of home-modified car can enter. According to Kevin Kennedy, a dirt-track enthusiast from Monroe, Louisiana, "One of the joys of attending a dirt-track race in the south, is getting covered with red dirt. There is so much of it that spectators wear goggles and VIPs sit behind Plexiglas for protection. When someone wins, the entire family—including the dog—gets down from the stands and sit on the car to do a victory lap."

DEMOLITION DERBIES

"People are always blown away by how vicious the derby we put on is."—Todd Dube, driver and dent representative, Dent National Championships, Steubenville, Ohio

Demolition derbies are based on one simple rule: The last car running wins, and the point is to smash all your competition into oblivion. If you have a car to spare, what's to stop you?

MUDBOG RACING

This is a sport where people drive their trucks through serious mud-slicks to see who can get across the fastest . . . or get across at all. The National Mudbog Federation claims it has a green effect: "By churning up the swamps, bogging plays a vital role in invigorating the ecosystem of the wetlands." Maybe, but the Mid-Iowa Mudhead Association is probably more truthful when they say mudbogging is all about "big money and bragging rights."

Mudhead Rules
- The four-wheel drive in your vehicle must work.
- You must have a hitch for a tow chain.
- Any truck with tires not regulated for the highway must go in the "outlaw" class.
- Boxes and beds must be clean of trash and alcohol.

These rigs commonly have big, thick drive trains, extra-wide tires, and engines modified to sustain high rpms. And while being sober and having a front-wheel drive will get you in the race, to win it, you need to know your mud and your physics. Mudboggers use the hydroplaning effect of big spinning tires to stop them from sinking, while at the same time getting purchase on the mud with the tire cleats. The two principles involved here are traction and flotation:

- **Traction** is movement across the mud. The cleats in the tires grab the mud, and the more weight on the tread, the more traction you have. But if you have too much traction, the mud will stick in the cleats, and your tires will turn into useless "mud-donuts."

"While this is an annual event, it actually occurs two or three times a year— basically whenever the locals get rowdy enough and the farmer who owns the land feels like dousing his field with shed-loads of water." —Genevieve Watson
(photos by Genevieve Watson).

- **Flotation** is what keeps you on top of the mud. While traction depends on exerting pressure down on your tires, this is pointless if it causes your rig to sink. Flotation is what keeps the tires above the mud by reducing the weight per square inch of tire. This is achieved by using big, air-filled tires.

Getting the balance right between traction and flotation is essential to get you through the mud. But whatever kind of mud you're in, if you're ahead, be sure to throw a rooster tail (spin your tires, hurling back a furl of mud) on your competitors whenever possible.

SWAMPING

When the mud gets too wet and too deep, it's a swamp. Swamping has the same objective as mudbogging, except if you want a chance in hell to get across, you have to build yourself a boat/truck combo known as a "swamp buggy." Swamp buggies were first made in the forties out of old Jeeps and oversized tires. Designed to navigate the Everglades, these strange-looking homemade machines even have their own hall of fame.

"There are restrictions placed on the use of swamp buggies in various parts of the Everglades, but there are also some racetracks and private parks where these things zip around at incredibly high rates of speed." —Gregory H., Florida folklorist

LAWN MOWER RACES

"I heard about a guy who tried to cut the hedges at his house by holding up a lawn mower. . . . Of course the mower fell on his hand and cut it off."
—Marshall Dostal, comedian

Lawn mower races are about hauling ass on a modified drive-mower around a grass track at sixty miles an hour with the same foot-to-the-

floor, grit-in-your-eye attitude the early stock car racers had. And unlike the Winston Cup circuit, the races are cheap to enter, mowers can be salvaged from the junkyard, and, with some ingenuity, they can still be modified into motor monsters at home. Let's face it, some people just want to drive anything as fast as it will go, and lawn mowers are much cheaper than cars. Wayne S., a thirty-five-year-old contract laborer, bought his mower for $100 and installed brakes from an old snowmobile.

The National Lawn Mower Racing Championships were started in Indianapolis in 1992 as an April Fools' joke. But it got serious fast.

ABOVE AND BELOW: *A lawnmower race (photos by Trish Potenza).*

Mower Mods

"The biggest challenge is definitely keeping from flipping over.
You go too hot into the corner and not only can you take yourself out
but you have someone on your tail who could potentially run you over."

—TRISH "IRON MAIDEN" POTENZA,
Ohio Mower Racers and Dewberry Mudboggers

It's important to note that while you are racing, you are *not* cutting grass. The first modification necessary on racing mowers is removal of the blades so you won't get burgered out there on the track if you get run over. The second essential modification is removal of the governor on the engine so the thing can drive at full speed. USLMRA races are divided into classes ranging from "S Stock" to "Factory Experimental," with all sorts of different mods, but that's a start.

Some racers run with standard lawn mower brakes; others prefer go-cart brakes. The stock brakes work pretty well, but you need fresh brake pads every race. *Important Note*: Remove the brake locking mechanism, which holds the brake in the locked position (for when you are parked) before you start racing your mower. Leaving this mechanism on the mower while racing is a serious safety hazard because the brake could get bumped and lock up accidentally, sending the mower into a skid. For safety, most races also require that racers wear long sleeves, a helmet, and a neck brace.

Nowadays, John Deeres, Dynastars, Snappers, and Murrays can be found racing and drawing thousands of fans in Stillwater, Oklahoma; Buda, Texas; and everywhere in between.

ROTARY TILLER RACES

The World Championship Rotary Tiller Races are held each June in Emerson, Arkansas. But they're a poor substitute for lawn mowers. Even when motorcycle engines are installed, the tillers still can only go eighteen miles per hour and churn up so much dirt, you'll need to wear ski goggles to keep from going blind.

A double-decker car race (photo courtesy of Jason Twite).

DANCING CARS

This sport should be called "freestyle spine compression" or "low-rider suicide." These drivers juice their customs with ten car batteries and mega-hydraulic shocks so the trucks can leap up five feet into the air. Then they go out and dance.

In the "hopping for height" competition, the front suspension is used to make the trucks rear up while the back wheels remain on the ground. The highest jump wins.

In the "dancing" competition, cars hop, leap, rear, shake, and any other gyration the driver can pull off. The most outrageous style wins the competition, and, of course, any fires, sparks, auto dismemberments, and explosions win the roar of the crowd. Here are some classic moves:

- **The Pancake:** Make the car hop repeatedly on all four wheels at the same time, preferably until the overloaded shocks spark and catch on fire.

A double-decker car race (photo courtesy of Jason Twite).

- **The Earthquake:** Make the car hop repeatedly on all four wheels, but upon landing, let the hydraulics out completely so the body of the truck itself slams into the ground. Repeat until your truck breaks completely in half.

WORLD-CLASS SPECTATOR FUN

Think heavy metal. Think multiple car wrecks, towering explosions, and hour upon hour of intense horsepower appreciation. These guys don't fuck around.

Monster Trucks: The world's first monster truck was invented in the mid-'70s by Bob Chandler of Hazelwood, Missouri. He took the wheels off his front-wheel-drive Ford pickup and added sixty-six-

A school-bus race (photo courtesy of Jason Twite).

inch tires from a manure spreader. In 1981 he used one of these trucks to crush a car.

These days, monster trucks are built from the ground up and sponsored by the WWF. They can crush dozens of cars and then go after each other. But at a really classy monster truck event, there is more to see than simply these professional huge-wheeled truck crushers. You'll find a full range of other strange, more homegrown races.

Double-Decker Cars: These cars are two cars stacked on top of each other. The car on the bottom controls the gas and brake while the car on top controls the steering, but there is no communication allowed between the drivers when they race. So things can easily get out of control.

Gauntlet Race: A bus must complete eight laps without being incapacitated by five normal-sized cars bent on taking it out. Jason Twite, at www.midwestmonsters.com, describes the gauntlet race at the Midsummer Night Scream: "The first couple of laps were normal, with the usual bumping and shoving and throwing of pumpkins out the back window. On lap five the bus got spun-out big time and nearly flipped right there. But it got moving again and it looked like for the first time the bigger vehicle was going to complete the eight laps. But that theory was put to sleep as . . . the bus was bumped from behind and hooked a rut on the infield and flipped over! The bus was literally twenty feet from winning the race."

School Bus Races: Souped-up school busses race, hoping to make it out through the turn . . .

NASCAR

"For when the last words in the Star Spangled Banner are, 'Gentlemen, start your engines!'" —Anonymous

People who don't love NASCAR think it's either too simple—people driving around and around a track at ear-bleeding speeds until someone waves the checkered flag—or too complicated—a motorhead's dream of intricate mechanics, octane, horsepower, explosions, aerodynamics, and dozens and dozens of mysterious metal parts. But what is

it about the rumble of the raceway and the taste of beer and chili dogs that gets the ladies so lathered?

Fans understand that it is the ultimate endorsement of cracker ingenuity. It grew from turning nothing into something. It is the "fix-'er-up" ethic gone pro. It is dirt tracks slicked out into super speedways. And hometown daredevils turned into national heroes.

"Our first car was number 50
because we paid fifty dollars for it."
—LEONARD WOOD

"Driving a race car is like dancing
with a chain saw."
—CALE YARBOROUGH

"There aren't any new frontiers anymore, not even the moon. The only thing left
for these guys to do is to go a little deeper into that first turn."
—KEN SQUIER

"I guess the country needed the wildness of stock car racing.
I know the South did."—RICHARD PETTY

"Fireball Roberts, perhaps the most nearly perfect of all stock car drivers,
is dead and it is like awaking to find a mountain suddenly gone."
—MAX MUHLEMAN in the *Charlotte News*,
on Fireball Roberts's fatal stock car crash

"Working on these cars, I can work on them day and night and don't never get
tired or never fail my mind. A man ought to do what he wants to, if there's any
way, if that's what he's going to be happy at."
—DALE EARNHARDT

FESTIVALS, FAIRS, AND CELEBRATIONS

Even if you don't have a killer Honcho, there are other cheap thrills to be had. And if you don't have a Honcho, you're probably not going to shell out hundreds of bucks to go watch American Gladiators and WWFers pretend to fight, anyway. But while Livestock Quiz Bowl may not rival watching the Rock whup Captain Caveman's ass in the flesh, at least the fights it causes are real.

STATE FAIRS, COUNTY FAIRS, AND HARVEST FESTIVALS

Tallest cornstalk contests, frog-jumping contests, tall-tale-telling, Cornflake Queen crowning, turkey calling, duck calling, chicken clucking, rooster crowing, wood chopping, maize mazes, cow milking, beard growing, egg rolling, bubblegum blowing, chili cook-offs, checkers championships, biggest pumpkin/watermelon/potato, best pie . . . The fair is a long-standing agrarian tradition based on the local crops and livestock. In many places, it is the biggest thing that happens all year, and people really prepare for it. Fair runners and the local chambers of commerce have mastered the art of the fair and have managed even to turn animal husbandry into a game. Sponsored by the 4-H

Club and the Future Farmers of America, livestock shows and competitions are a centerpiece of the fairs . . .

COWS

"You want your bulls to be masculine and your cows to be feminine—just like humans."—Aaron Grant, Calgary Stampede judge

The ideal cow has a well-developed (but not too pronounced) muscle structure and shows fat deposits on its forerib, brisket, and crop but very little around its tailhead. The rump should be wide and slightly sloped and should look wedge-shaped from the top as well as the sides. Then the judges will say, "This is a nice heifer with not too many holes in her."

She should have a tight udder, and the teats should be close together. Make sure her legs and feet are in good shape ("She's clean in the hock") and that she walks without listing to one side ("handles her legs"), and doesn't look like she's about to fall flat on her face. When the judges say she "walks a little bit downhill," it's all over.

Fainting Goats

The famous Tennessee Fainting Goats have a condition called *myotonia congenitia*, which means their muscle cells freeze up when they are startled, so they fall down. Fainting goats trace back to a man named Tinsley, who brought them to Tennessee around 1880. He used fainting goats as part of his medicine show to hawk a fake "reviving" potion to swooning Victorian ladies. Of course, the ladies didn't know that the goats would come to with or without the elixir.

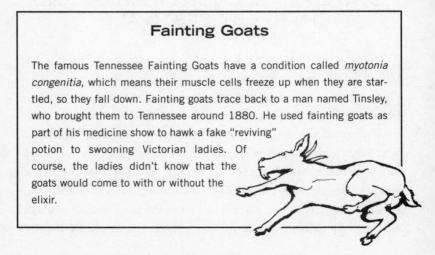

Alternative Cow Events

- **Cow Chip Throwing:** For nineteenth-century pioneers, throwing cow chips meant having some fuel to burn for the coming winter. The settlers needed to stave off the severe prairie weather and discovered that dried buffalo chips burned hot and clean. But when all the buffalo got killed off, the settlers had to make do with burning smelly cow chips instead. Each fall the family spent a day in the fields chucking chips into the wagon. Then it got to be all about "who could throw farther" and "who got better spin," and people started bragging and all that, so a competition was arranged . . . The World Cow Chip Throwing Championships are still held annually in Beaver, Oklahoma, as proof that with a little ingenuity, even throwing shit can be made into a game. It is accompanied at some fairs by a rubber chicken throwing contest.

The cow-chip-throwing world record is held by Leland Searcy, who threw a chip 182 feet and 3 inches, in 1979. The women's world record was set at the Luckenbach World's Fair, Fredricksburg, Texas, in 1976 by Patty Edwards: "I won a huge, huge, huuuuuge cow chip sprayed with gold paint. It was in a frame and all that, and they presented it to me in front of 10,000 people. It was the greatest day of my life."

Chip-Tossing Rules in Beaver

- Two chips per person. Furthest toss counts.
- If the chip busts up in the air, the furthest flying piece counts as your throw distance.
- You must pick your chips from the Chamber of Commerce Wagon (no private loads allowed).
- Altering the shape of your chip costs you a twenty-five-foot penalty.
- Chips must be over six inches in diameter, and throwers must be over sixteen.

- **Bullshit Bingo:** Sometimes referred to by the more genteel as "cow patty bingo," bullshit bingo is basically a bull wandering around on a grid of numbers and if he takes a shit on your number, you win.

This Little Piggy Went to Market

Three genetically altered pigs were stolen from the University of Florida and showed up as sausages served at a funeral in High Springs. The hogs were supposed to have been incinerated, but an animal technician admitted to stealing their bodies. One ended up in the hands of the butcher who said the meat "didn't taste right." Maybe because the hogs had been altered and injected with enough chemicals to kill a . . . well, 500-pound pig.

This Little Piggy Stayed Home

In Texas, a rule at major livestock shows is that pigs are only allowed to be shown once. But Cammy Cornelius wanted to show her prize pig—which won top honors and $4,000 at the St. Angeleno Livestock Show—again. The pig was sold to a slaughterhouse at the fair but never made it there: the authorities said it was stolen.

The pig resurfaced a few months later at another fair and was recognized right before it was about to win another award. The police alleged that Cammy and her dad had stolen the pig back from the slaughterhouse. Indicted on charges of third-degree organized criminal activity, Cammy got one year of probation and a $1,000 fine for making false statements to a grand jury, and her dad got three years of probation and a $3,000 fine for his false testimony (the fines exactly equaling the money the prize pig won the first time around).

PIGS

Raising a champion pig isn't about shoveling them a lot of snacks. Contestants need to keep a record of the feed they use, of expenses, and of the pig's growth and back-fat percentages. Champion hogs are walked only in the shade, trained to respond to stick prodding, and massaged with aloe vera and sunscreen. Paul R., a high school senior, raised a Chesapeake Jubilee Champion hog and said he spent 4.5 hours of work per day with his pigs to prepare them for the show.

Judges nowadays are looking for leaner, longer hogs. A prizewinning pig should have more muscle than fat; if the ratio is right, the pig should be walking nice and wide on strong, thick hams. If the pig's top half is a lot wider than its bottom half, it's too fat. A pig should have big square feet and take long strides. Otherwise, there's probably something wrong with its shoulders or hips, and though it might bulge with back fat, it will never be jock enough to really bulk up the hams. *Hint:* When picking a piglet to be your prize hog, look for a long one. A longer pig means a delay in the development of a pig's fat deposits, which means *more meat*.

PONIES

The 4-H Club runs horse shows for teenagers. They judge grooming, hoof picking, stall cleaning, and tack maintenance, as well as jumping and riding competitions called gymkhanas, which test the rider's skills with games like riding while balancing an egg on a spoon or a dollar bill clenched against the saddle at the knee. The last rider with the egg or the dollar wins. But while gymkhana games might suffice for the 4-Hers, the men-from-the-boys crowd will most likely hit up the broncs at the rodeo.

RODEO

"I don't have freckles anymore; I reckon the bulls shook them all off."
—Freckles Brown, champion bull rider

Though there seems to be no ranch work that requires riding a psychotic bull, rodeos are often part of state fairs and are designed to show off a cowboy's skills at roping cattle, training cow ponies, wrestling steers, and breaking broncs.

Red Rock, the most famous bull in rodeo history, died at the age of eighteen in 1994. He was a red brindle, a cross-bred bull born in Oregon and named after a formation of red rocks near his ranch. At the age of two, Red Rock was sold to Mert Hunking, a rodeo stock contractor who realized the bull had an innate instinct for what a bull rider was going to do and always went the other way. Before he was through, Red Rock threw every champion bull rider on the circuit.

But if you're not animally inclined, and you don't feel like participating in another Livestock Quiz Bowl, you could provide a clogging accompaniment to a mean fiddler's tune.

A musician playing a washtub base at Mardi Gras.

MUSIC

People may show off their talents at bluegrass festivals but cut their teeth at state fairs, where they can enter contests in the 18 and under, 18 to 50, and 50+ categories for piano, harmonica, kazoo, accordion, banjo, guitar, mandolin, and fiddling. But sometimes people make their own instruments:

- **Carpenter's Saw:** To add a spooky wobbling voice to your song, take an ordinary carpenter's saw. Clamp the handle between your knees, hold the tip with one hand, and bend it into an "S" shape. Draw a bow across the smooth side of the saw with the other hand. The saw will sing to you, and by bending the tip back and forth, you can vary the pitch and make it wobble.
- **Gong:** To make a gong that can be heard for miles, hang a railroad tie by one end from a crossbeam so it vibrates. Hit it with a sledgehammer, and you'll be calling all the dogs in for dinner. Another industrial gong can be made by hanging the blade of a circular saw.
- **Violin:** Make your own violin with a broom, a pail, some fishing line, and a bow. Put the broom, sweeper side up, into the pail. Tie the fishing line from the pail to the head of the broom. Tilt the broom back and forth to vary the pitch of the string, run your bow across it, and you're making music. You can do the same for a bass using a metal washtub, a weed whacker, and a two-by-four.
- **Drums:** To add percussion, bang a drumstick across a washboard.

The First Electric Guitar

The electric guitar was invented in the thirties by two musicians, George Beauchamp and Paul Barth. The pickup was made out of two horseshoe magnets and a coil they wound around the motor from Beauchamp's washing machine, which they later replaced with a motor from a sewing machine. Harry Watson, the plant superintendent at National Guitar Company, carved the neck and body of that first electric guitar in a few hours at Beauchamp's kitchen table, using all hand tools. The guitar worked, but they called it the "Frying Pan" because it looked more like a skillet than a guitar.

LOCAL FESTIVALS

"If we didn't have the 'Chitlin' Strut,' we would have to double our taxes."
—Mayor R. N. "Bob" Salley, Salley, South Carolina

People want something to do, and festivals give them a reason to come out, get drunk, and spend money. So small towns become the "world capital" of a major local product for the weekend, throw a fair in its honor, and make money. Forty thousand people come for chitterlings in Salley, South Carolina. Over the weekend, they eat 10,000 pounds of fried pig intestines and clear $25,000 for the town. Springfield, South Carolina, has repaired aging sewer and water lines with profits from the annual governor's frog jump and egg-striking contest. Festivals are also held in the name of catfish, peanuts, pickles, watermelons, onions, chickens, garlic, grits, and blossoming fruit trees. But sometimes too many places claim a world-class title . . .

BARBECUE COOK-OFFS

While the **Big Pig Jig** is Georgia's "official" BBQ championship cook-off and is known as the "Redneck Mardi Gras," only the winners of the BPJ even qualify to enter the Memphis in May competition.

Memphis in May is *one* of the biggest BBQ competitions in the world, hosting the World Championship BBQ cooking contest (strictly pork), with such formidable teams as "Pork, Sweat, and Beers" and "A*porc*alypse Now." The top prize is

THE SECRET TO A CLEAN PIG

"The heel strings were cut on each of the hog's hind legs . . . and the hog dragged to the huge cast-iron boiler, which sat in a depression dug into the ground so the hog could be slipped in and pulled out easily . . . The fire had to be tended carefully because the water could never quite come to a boil. If the hog was dipped in boiling water, the hair would set and become impossible to take off. The ideal temperature was water you could rapidly draw your finger through three times in succession without being blistered . . . After the hog is pulled from the water, a blunt knife is drawn over the animal, and if the water has not been too hot, the hair slips off smooth as butter, leaving a white, naked, utterly beautiful pig."

—HARRY CREWS, *A Childhood: Biography of a Place*

a five-foot trophy crowned with a statue of four kneeling pigs and a large meat cleaver hanging over all their little heads.

But **The American Royal Barbecue Championship** in Kansas City, Missouri, is *the* biggest BBQ competition in the world, known as the "Superbowl of Barbecue." Contenders must have won at least one major nationally recognized BBQ competition to apply and then must be accepted. If you win the "right" competitions, you'll certainly qualify as a contender for the American Royal.

RATTLESNAKE ROUNDUP

"A lot of people want to see somebody get bit, just like they want to go to a car race to see a wreck."—Ken Garrett, rattlesnake handler, New Mexico

The fascination with rattlers draws out thousands of hunters and spectators to rattlesnake roundups every year. The official hunting season starts in New Mexico in March and then heads East: The Whigan, Georgia, roundup is held the last Saturday in January. One of the largest roundups is held in Okeene, Oklahoma, where 100,000 pounds of live and deadly diamondbacks are turned in during the two-day event.

Snakebite

A snake hunter's rule of thumb is that a snake can only strike a distance of half its length, but even so, if you get bit:

- Stay still and keep the wounded area down below your heart.
- Have someone go for help. There are antidotes at the hospital.
- To slow blood flow, you can wrap a bandage two to four inches above the bite, but the Red Cross says *no tourniquets*.
- Do not try to cauterize the bite or cut into it.
- If you get a chance to kill the snake, bring it to the hospital so the doctors will know exactly what kind of venom they're treating.

After the snakes are caught at a roundup, they're cooked up, but take an Oklahoma snake butcher's advice: "You got to handle the snakes with care. They can pee 360 degrees and can be deadly for up to two hours after they are dead." (Don't get bit. Go to p. 62.)

Rattlesnack

"At Carl Allen's restaurant in Auburndale, Florida, you sat at tables that once were sewing machines, drank ice tea from fruit jars and could order (in addition to rattlesnake) fried rabbit, armadillo, mullet, turtle, catfish, and even ordinary chicken and cornbread." —Al Burt, *The Tropic of Cracker*

Snake meat
Flour
1 egg
1 tsp. Tabasco
1 splash milk
½ cup cornmeal
1 tsp. herbs (sage, rosemary, and thyme good)
½ tsp. each salt and pepper
Vegetable oil

Roll snake meat in flour. Dip in mixture of egg, Tabasco, and milk. Roll in mixture of cornmeal, herbs, salt, and pepper. Fry in oil until crispy. Serve with cocktail sauce or tartar sauce.

How to Clean Your Snake

1. Take the *dead* rattlesnake, cut off head and throw it away, *carefully*: The reflexes in the jaw work for hours after the snake is dead, so it can still bite. But all the venom is contained in two sacks in the rattler's head, and once the head is gone, so is the poison.
2. Hold the cutting edge of the knife facing out to avoid puncturing any organs, and slice down the middle of the belly, neck to tail.
3. Grab the skin at the neck end, and peel back.
4. Scrape out internal organs. And get the meat on ice ASAP.

Some claim you can make a self-stirring chili by putting the whole snake in the pot while it's still alive and cook it: The wriggling of the snake will stir the chili. Ingenuity to some, but then again, you might well cook the venom into your food.

HISTORICAL FAIRS

Places that may not get to claim that they are the onion or pickle or locust bean capital of the world often have fairs to celebrate their history, instead. From annual "Remember the Alamo!" reenactments to reviving the Pony Express, people will dig up anything for a reason to party.

Pioneer Parties: Lots of states honor our brave, hairy, possum-shooting frontiersmen and home-steader ancestors who trekked thousands of miles to settle the West. Malvern, Ohio, hosts the **Great Trail Days** at the end of the summer; Corpus Christi, Texas, has **Buccaneer Days** in the spring; and Red Hills State Park in Illinois offers two days of "living history" during April's **Old Settler Days**. There are dozens of Frontier Days festivals out there celebrating the survival and wilderness skills used by our forefathers and mothers in the great back of beyond. The biggest of these is held in Cheyenne, Wyoming, and features special guest characters like Lilly Langree, Doc Holiday, Big Nose Kate, and Wyatt Earp. And, in addition to the requisite rodeo, stampede, old-time music, ragpicking, traditional storytelling, clogging, and whiskey swilling, Frontier Days include such indispensables as tomahawk throwing and anvil shooting.

Tomahawk Throwing: Most people think of tomahawks as an Indian thing, but they were used extensively by the pioneers, who got pretty good at throwing them, usually at dinner, but sometimes at each other. Every year, at the **Old Settler Days** in Malvern, Ohio, the Buffalo Trace Muzzleloaders Association puts on a tomahawk-throwing exhibition. Other festivals, like the **Oak Ridge Festival** in Willard, Ohio, stage competitions for which people practice all year.

Contestants throw the tomahawk at the "hawk block," which is usually a large tree stump, and are required to prove their skill by doing precision exercises like throwing the tomahawk so that it slices through a playing card pinned to the block. Another favorite is the string/egg game. A string with an egg tied to the end of it is hung near the top of the block. The players must cut the string without breaking the egg. If they miss the string or break the egg, some judges make them eat the raw egg right then and there.

Anvil Shooting: Yes, anvils: 100 to 200 pounds of steel shot about thirty feet into the air with gunpowder. Some claim this game started back in the Gold Rush days, when miners would test their powder by shooting anvils, and it evolved into something of a competition. Maybe that's true, or perhaps the miners just needed to

PROJECTILE FOOD

Betty Cracker's got her own idea of fun . . .

Potato Cannons

With a barrel and chamber made out of PVC pipes, a potato stuffed down the barrel for ammunition, and hair spray sparked by a gas barbecue igniter for firepower, potato cannons are a classic cheap thrill. But even in their simplest form, a potato cannon can have a range of 300 feet with a potato velocity of ninety miles an hour—so duck and cover.

Aquanet Fishing Artillery

Clever fishermen looking for extra range also employ devices similar to potato cannons, only they call them "surf-casting cannons" and use them to fire a fishing line attached to an orange or grapefruit (which also acts as a buoy) up to 1,200 feet out into the open water.

Punkin' Chunkin'

Punkin' Chunkin' proves you don't need hair spray to launch edible projectiles. The object of chunking is to use a catapult to hurl ten-pound pumpkins as far as possible without resorting to explosives. And it's no casual matter at the World Championship Punkin' Chunkin' Contest in Delaware where people build monster chunkers which are like giant pea shooters, powered with compressed air. They can shoot pumpkins at speeds up to 500 miles an hour. One chunker, "Big 10 Inch," has a 100-foot barrel made from an aluminum irrigation pipe. Another is powered by a pressurized gas made by mixing liquid nitrogen with boiling water. But it was the "Aludium Q36 Pumpkin Modulator" out of Iowa that once chunked a pumpkin 4,026 feet.

Graffiti Eggs

Taggers looking to mark something they can't reach with a spray can sometimes use graffiti eggs to get a long range advantage. They drain the eggs through a small hole, and then, using a syringe, refill the egg with paint. When the eggs hit the wall, they smash, leaving blossoms of paint on the target. There's great evidence of graffiti egging on the hard-to-reach parts of the Longfellow Bridge in Boston, Massachusetts.

Hot-dog Missiles

At baseball games, people love to try to catch flying baseballs and at the Philadelphia Phillies' home stadium they can try to catch a free lunch. The team's mascot, the green Phillie Phanatic, uses a three-foot-long tube to fire wrapped hot dogs a hundred feet into the stands.

burn off some excess testosterone. But members of the World Anvil Shooting Society claim that shooting anvils started during the Civil War, when Northern troops tried to blow up Southern anvils to reduce their steel supplies. Either way, there is a National Anvil Shooting Contest held in Laurel, Mississippi, every year.

AND THEN THERE ARE FESTIVALS FOR THE FAMOUS...

Authentic Bonnie and Clyde Festival: A reenactment of Bonnie and Clyde's last ride is staged every year near the end of May in Gibsland, Louisiana, where Bonnie and Clyde stopped to eat their last

meal at Canfield's Café on May 23, 1934. They were driving to the nearby Methvin Farm to meet a member of their gang when they were ambushed and killed in a bullet storm. When the corpses were pulled from the car, Bonnie and Clyde each had more than forty bullet holes in their bodies, and Bonnie was still clutching her sandwich. "We draw from 3,000 to 5,000 visitors every year," says seventy-year-old Billie Jean Pollard, the chairwoman of the reenactment committee. People come from all over the world, she says. "They can't hear or see or learn enough about those two."

Tom Sawyer Days: The biggest event at the summer Tom Sawyer Days held in Mark Twain's hometown of Hannibal, Missouri, is the National Fence-Painting Contest, open to boys ages ten to thirteen.

Started in 1956 and inspired by the clever Tom Sawyer, who conned his friends into whitewashing the whole of his Aunt Polly's fence while he watched, this competition now takes only one "fence-painting champion" from each of the ten states that border the Mississippi River.

Wyatt Earp Days: Every Memorial Day weekend, Tombstone, Arizona, "the town too tough to die," throws a festival in memory of Wyatt Earp, Doc Holliday, and the infamous gunfight at the OK Corral. The gunfight reenactments are done by the Tombstone Renegade Lions and the Tombstone Vigilantes. And for those who prefer to show how tough they are inside, there is the supremely spicy chili cook-off.

GETTING WEIRD

When you are neither the sarsaparilla capital of the world nor the home of the Alamo, and you want to have a festival, sometimes you just have to get weird . . .

Roswell UFO Encounter Festival: In 1947, in the Land of Enchantment, an unidentified flying object crashed on Hub Corn's sheep ranch just outside Roswell. It became a famous "national secret" and every year now, hundreds of alien enthusiasts (and abductees) gather there on July Fourth weekend to wait for the mothership.

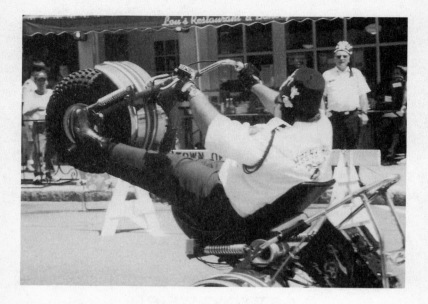

Shriner Parades: They race tractors, fit snowmobiles onto wheels, build mini cars and motorized tricycles, and practice their parade formations for months. Shriners are part of the Ancient Arabic Order of the Nobles of the Mystic Shrine for North America, which explains their red fezzes. Their parades help fund a bunch of children's hospitals, which they call "the heart and soul of the Shrine." Similar, though less pageant-oriented, philanthropic organizations include the Rotary Club, and the Lion's Club . . .

National Hobo Convention: It started in 1900 as a joke when the editor of a rural Iowa newspaper wrote that there was going to be a hobo convention in Britt, Iowa. A bunch of reporters went to the site to cover the event and found that no one was there. Not to be outdone, they published a bunch of made-up stories about the "wild event." The hoax became so famous that the following year a bunch of hoboes actually *did* show up in Britt, and the convention's been held every year since.

Rock City Fairy-tale Festival: About six miles outside Chattanooga, Tennessee, Rock City is a natural rock formation on Lookout Mountain that was transformed during the Depression into a "magical garden" for tourists, filled with swinging bridges, wildflowers, and dozens of cement gnomes. The surrounding area became known as Fairyland and hosts a fairy tale–telling festival every year.

Annual RC Cola and MoonPie Festival: A classic combination, a cold RC Cola and a MoonPie, were standard lunch fare for sharecroppers until the 1970s. But the combo is still celebrated every year in Bell Buckle, Tennessee (*not* the manufacturing home of either), where people play MoonPie Hoops, MoonPie Stacking, and MoonPie Toss, and share the "World's Largest MoonPie."

Mashed-Potato Wrestling: At the Annual Potato Blossom Festival in Fort Fairfield, Maine, people wrestle in mashed potatoes. The festival lasts for eight days and draws about 35,000 people who, by the end of the week, have wrestled in 700 pounds of watered-down coarse-grind potato flour.

And Don't Forget . . . In Oatman, Arizona, there is an **egg-frying contest** every Fourth of July, where contestants use aluminum foil and magnifying glasses to fry eggs in the desert sun. And the weirdness goes on. . . . People race couches and toilets down a ski slope in Whitefish, Montana, during the **Big Mountain Furniture Race.** In Nome, Alaska, bathers in bathtubs race down Main Street. Then there's **The Dukes of Hazard Fan Club Convention** and the **Bald Is Beautiful Annual Convention**. But the weirdness centerfold goes to the Redneck Games.

The Redneck Games

"Rednecks have fun a little differently from everybody else. How many people do you know who would bob for pig feet? It's not something you'd do at your family reunion."—Mark Powers, WQZY deejay

The Redneck Games were dreamed up by Mac Davis, general manager of WQZY radio station in Dublin, Georgia (pop 16,000), as a station stunt during the 1996 Atlanta Olympic Games. Jeff Foxworthy had recently commented that organizers wouldn't be able to light the Olympic flame in Atlanta without someone trying to

Redneck Games trophy
(photo courtesy of
Mark Powers).

roast a pig over it. Further inspiration was a set of cracker ingenuity–style Olympic rings made from five old bicycle tires, spray-painted the Olympic colors, and hung on Main Street in nearby Aline. The event was originally called the Redneck Olympic Games, but the organizers were forced to drop "Olympic" because the Atlanta Olympic Games Committee did not wish to be associated.

Each year, the Redneck Games raise thousands of dollars for Shriner's Children's Hospitals, and the Shriners helped make it happen—Shriners from as far as Savannah and Macon. The South Georgia Redneck Queen usually comes, too.

The games begin when a local named Elbow lights the ceremonial BBQ with the ceremonial torch, a blowtorch sheathed in a tube of Budweiser cans. But organizers decided to skip the symbolic "releasing the doves of peace" part, for fear someone might shoot the birds right out of the sky. What do you win? Trophies mounted with crumpled Bud cans and medallions made from crushed cans painted gold.

While a wet T-shirt contest was nixed out of good taste, and greased-pig wrestling and cow tipping were rejected for safety reasons, there are plenty of other games:

- Bobbing for Pig's Feet: Contestants have thirty seconds to pick as many pig's feet as possible out of a bucket of water—with their teeth.
- Mud-Pit Belly Flop: The prize goes to the person who can slop the most specta-

tors with red Georgia mud. Size is an advantage in this game.

- Hubcap Hurl: Throw a hubcap instead of the discus.
- Armpit Serenade: This appeals mainly to teenage boys who like to make farting noises with their armpits. Favorite tunes are "Old Macdonald Had a Farm" and the theme from *Green Acres*.
- Okonee River Raft Race: This was brought back as part of the Redneck Games in 2000 after the race had been discontinued in town fifteen years earlier because people were getting "drunk and sexy" on the water. The raft race is the place for crackers to flex their ingenuity muscle. While some float downriver in kayaks, canoes, and rubber rafts, the

Redneck Games champion (photo courtesy of Mark Powers).

diehards rise to the challenge: a Volkswagen car body floating on oil drums, an outhouse converted into a pedal boat, a ripped-off trailer porch held up by Clorox bottles. . . .

Bike-tire Olympic rings (photo courtesy of Mark Powers).

Discontinued Events

- The Cigarette-Butt Flip was discontinued after the first year because officials discovered a fishing weight shoved inside the farthest-flicked butt after it suspiciously went twice as far as all the others and because a twelve-year-old wanted to enter, claiming he was an excellent butt flipper.
- The Bottle-Throw-at-Stop-Sign game was also put to rest in 1996, not because it inspired twelve-year-olds to delinquency but because a woman threw her longneck straight through WQZY's satellite dish while trying to hit the sign.
- The Big Hair Competition also only made it for one year (see page 93).

"It's supposed to be a family day. . . . It's not unlike being at the beach . . . You just don't have the ocean."—Mark Powers, WQZY deejay

Vices

There are hundreds of ways to get fucked up. And enterprising crackers understand that there's no need to give fistfuls of cash to unreliable junkies with handguns just to get off. Those with the will, if not the means, have found ways to bypass the international drug cartels with this unique class of vices, which can be cooked up right off the discount-store shelf. This isn't in here to tell the DEA to pull NyQuil from the shelves because some people chug it red, but to show that people will stop at nothing to relieve boredom.

Photo by Genevieve Watson

UNDER THE COUNTER

SPEED

The pursuit of "speed" involves modifying increasingly regulated over-the-counter medicines. Amphetamines were first made in Germany in 1887 as a bronchodilator/vasoconstrictor to relieve hay fever, asthma, and allergies. But the Germans discovered an important side effect: Amphetamines increase physical and mental acuity and "cause wakefulness," which is where the trouble comes in and why amphetamines became known as *speed*.

During World War II, amphetamine tablets were used to keep pilots awake on their return from bombing raids. And rumor has it Hitler was injected daily with methamphetamine, a brutally strong form of amphetamine invented in Japan in 1919. He may have been the world's first speed freak.

Meanwhile, back on the home front, amphetamines came in a variety different flavors:

BENZEDRINE (Laevoamphetamine)

Ladies at home had "bennies," or "pep" pills, to keep their energy up to rally around the hearth. And in 1932, the benzedrine inhaler was introduced by Smith Kline & French as an over-the-counter asthma medicine. But clever speed freaks soon figured out how to break open the inhaler and get at the benzedrine-soaked insert inside. They would soak it in soda, which they would then drink. (It contained the equivalent of fifty-six amphetamine tablets.) A favorite of Jack Kerouac, it allowed him to stay awake for days. But as an FDA trial loomed in 1949, the manufacturers removed the inhaler from the shelves.

DEXEDRINE (Dextroamphetamine)

Dexedrine became an active ingredient in diet pills—"dexies," "fire reds," "Christmas trees"—after it was discovered that, in addition to pepping you up, it kept the weight off. Dexedrine was also used on ADHD kids to help them to concentrate and was thus readily available for abuse.

The '40s were the golden age of amphetamine use. According to Lester Grinspoon, a professor of psychiatry at Harvard Medical School, "Physicians were the major agents for overuse of amphetamines . . . physicians really believed it was like a panacea and that there was no downside." But in 1955, California Superior Court Judge

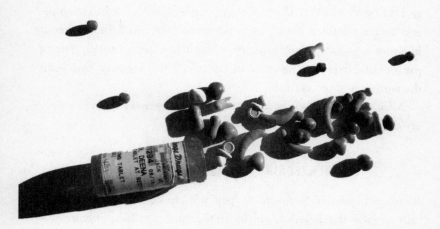

Twain Michelson warned Congress that amphetamines were a part of the "red menace," and part of China's secret plan to subvert the West. All amphetamines were made illegal with the U.S. Drug Abuse Regulation and Control Act of 1970.

Even in their new, harder-to-get state, amphetamines are still thought to be superior to cocaine in the uppers crowd in three major ways: (1) They can be taken orally. Cocaine has to be injected or sniffed, which isn't good for your nose. (2) The high lasts much longer. (3) It's cheap.

CRYSTAL METH (Methamphetamine)

Methedrine, meth, crystal . . . It's the strongest of the amphetamines and the crown jewel of the homemade amphetamine scene. It's cheap and long lasting: Meth users say it helps them work long shifts and get it on for hours. A speed tweaker's dream, it can keep him alert and paranoid for days on end, and it is still commonly sold on the black market today.

- **Advantage:** You'll be dancing on the ceiling for days.
- **Disadvantage:** You'll be dancing on the ceiling for days.
- **Disadvantage:** Bikers promoted meth and gave it the nickname "crank" in the '60s because they used to hide it in the crankcases of their bikes. And since serious tweakers often hallucinate that bugs are crawling beneath their skin, they call them crank bugs.

- **Disadvantage:** *Crystal meth psychosis* is the clinical term for losing it, when reality takes a holiday and hallucinations, paranoia, and "bizzare compulsions" like painting a house with a toothbrush for fourteen hours solid take over. (Luckily, this usually doesn't happen unless you've been awake for at least five days straight.)

By 1970 the feds had made all amphetamines illegal, but by then speed fiends had learned how to manufacture their own meth by cooking up some really scary ingredients. It takes three days to make, stinks worse than a methane refinery, and is highly explosive, but most of the essential ingredients might live right under the sink. (Go to p. 190, and/or go to p. 62.)

- **P2P Meth, aka "Philly Meth":** This kind of meth is increasingly rare but considered the strongest kind around. It's ingredients include lye, battery acid, and P2P (phenyl-2-propane), a solvent used to clean swimming pools. P2P is no longer legal in the U.S. but is still legal elsewhere.
- **Ephedrine Meth, aka "California Meth":** Ephedrine is one atom different from methamphetamine and is sometimes known as "trucker speed." While it has become increasingly restricted, its synthetic double, pseudoephedrine, is available over the counter in medicines like Sudafed. Both can be combined with other chemicals to make meth. Large quantities of ephedrine/pseudoephedrine can be purified and converted to meth using household ingredients like gasoline additives, rubbing alcohol, drain cleaner, distilled water, lye, and coffee filters.

Meth comes in other forms made with the same gritty battery-acid and Drano aesthetic—CAT, ICE . . . —but you get the idea. Enough.

Making Coffee Without Coffee Beans

During the Civil War, people figured out how to make coffee substitutes using boiled, parched rye; brown-roasted English peas; and ground grape seeds.

During World War II, Postum, a cereal-based coffee substitute invented by Charles W. Post, was widely used. The first batch of Postum was made with wheat, bran, and molasses using a gas stove, a peanut roaster, and a coffee grinder. Some people who suffer from stomach problems still drink Postum, but otherwise everyone's back to coffee because it has what all the substitutes lack: *caffeine*.

OVER-THE-COUNTER TRUCKER SPEED

Ephedrine, or pseudoephedrine, which is still available over the counter, is also known as trucker speed, blasting caps, Mini-Thins, and white crosses. It has now replaced amphetamines as a bronchodilater and can also be used to make California-style methamphetamine.

Because pseudoephedrine can be found in products like Sudafed and Robitussin, the DEA imposed new rules in 1996 regulating over-the-counter sales of cold medicines. Some states have banned over-the-counter sales of all ephedrine/pseudoephedrine products, while others still offer them but restrict bulk sales to keep people from making crystal meth.

But even if the feds decided to take all the ephedrine/pseudoephedrine products off the market, thus infuriating millions of cold sufferers daily, a natural form of ephedrine known as "ephedra" comes from a Chinese herb used to treat bronchial ailments called "ma huang." The world's oldest known medicine, it is a major ingredient in herbal ecstasy and will no doubt provide plenty of fodder for the next generation of speed seekers.

CAFFEINE

No-Doz, Vivarin, Penguin caffeinated mints . . . People crush them, snort them, and dissolve them in beer to keep awake for an all-night party. Once again, where there's a will . . .

A case of the effects of extreme caffeine consumption was reported in 1936 in the *New England Journal of Medicine*. The patient took a bunch of caffeine pills before going to a party. "She became silly, elated, and euphoric." As hours passed she scarfed the entire box of pills, which amounted to about 1,800 milligrams of pure caffeine. (FYI: A twelve-ounce Coke contains 45 milligrams of caffeine). "She became confused, disoriented, excited, restless, and violent, shouted and screamed and began to throw things about her room." The article goes on to describe how this normally quiet and religious woman was cursing and using profane language, and then collapsed and was taken to the hospital. The staff couldn't figure out what was wrong with her and sent her home. About a month later she ate another box of caffeine pills and was again taken to the hospital. This time they stuck her in a psych ward. Eventually, nurses noticed she was drinking an inordinate amount of coffee. When they confiscated the coffee, her behavior returned to normal, and she was discharged.

TRANQUILIZERS

GEORGIA HOME BOY

GHB, Grievous Bodily Harm, Liquid X, Scoop, Goop, Gamma-oh . . . Gamma hydroxybutyrate is a nervous-system depressant that

ELVIS THE PELVIS

Elvis, who was popping tranquilizers and barbiturates for much of his life, actually wrote a letter to Nixon in 1970 offering his services to work for the feds as an undercover agent in drug enforcement. *Spin* magazine listed the 100 sleaziest moments in rock history and this one made #15: "Elvis inquires about becoming an honorary DEA agent; President Richard Nixon gives him the badge."

was used as an anesthetic in Europe. It was sold in U.S. health food stores after bodybuilders claimed it helped their muscles grow. But vicelings quickly figured out that if you took a bunch of GHB, you'd get a buzz. It was cheap, readily available, and wouldn't get you a DUI on the way home. But the FDA caught on and included it in Schedule I of the Controlled Substances Act in 2000. So now it's as expensive, difficult to get, and as dangerous to use as the most potent street drugs. (So if you get caught go to p. 190.)

HORSE TRANQUILIZERS

People take Ketamine, which is a horse tranquilizer. If you take too much, you can tumble down a K hole and won't be able to move for hours.

HUFFING AND SNIFFING

"There was another kid at the party as in love with Milly as I was, but Milly assured me that he held no interest for her. She had heard that he sometimes crawled up on the refund-gas tank—which stored the tax-free gasoline allotted to the farmers for farm machinery—and inhaled the fumes until he passed out, and fell off the tank and injured himself."—Lewis Nordan, *Boy With Loaded Gun*

SNIFFERS inhale through nose.

HUFFERS inhale through mouth.

Huffing and sniffing gasoline and the like deprive your brain of oxygen.

- **Advantage:** You get an instant intense high. (Inhalants aren't called "deliriants" for nothing.)
- **Disadvantage**: It's a very short-lived high, kills a lot of brain cells, and can also kill the rest of you. You could suffocate, be poisoned by the fumes, or go into cardiac arrest. Take your pick. (Go to p. 62.)

HUFFING AEROSOLS

People huff spray paint, deodorant, and hair spray to get the fluorocarbon rush. They spray the aerosol into a balloon or a bag and breathe in. But even with something as "wholesome" as cooking spray, people have managed to kill themselves.

SNIFFING GLUE

Sniffers empty tubes of hobby glue into baggies and sniff sharply for a hallucinogenic effect: "Imagine brick walls opening in slow motion" (Debbie X). The first recorded cases of glue-sniffing in this country were reported in 1959 by the *Denver Post*, when a bunch of teenagers were discovered with their hands covered with model airplane glue, which they were inhaling deeply. The organic solvents in "hobby glue," mostly toluene, are what give you the rush. People also huff White-Out and rubber cement.

IDIOT BOX

One girl died from huffing insecticide. Sad, but . . . *duh*.

"I remember a bottle of rubber cement broke in my backpack once in high school. I wore the backpack over my head like a hat for about a minute. . . . I caught an absolute monster buzz, had to leave class and roam the halls for about twenty minutes to get my sanity back."—Marshall Dostal

LAUGHING GAS

Nitrous oxide produces a huffer's high and also kills pain, which is why dentists use it. Also known as "hippie crack," the gas is dispensed from a nitrous oxide tank into a balloon and huffed.

- **Advantage:** It's quicker than getting drunk and only lasts for a few minutes.
- **Disadvantage:** Federal law mandates that nitrous can only be sold to legitimate users, which include dentists, hospitals, clinics, gas repackagers, and distributors.

IDIOT BOX

People try to eliminate the balloon middleman and suck nitrous right out of the tank. This can easily freeze your lungs and adiós to you.

WHIPPED-CREAM WHIPPETS

The gas behind whippets is CO_2, and people either suck it off Reddi-Whip cans or buy CO_2 cartridges (sold to make homemade whipped cream and soda water) and a "cracker," to break the cartridge seal. Fearless whippet seekers have been known to huff whipped-cream cans right off the supermarket shelf.

ETHER

"This is the main advantage of ether: it makes you behave like the village drunkard in some early Irish novel . . . total loss of all basic motor skills: blurred vision, no balance, numb tongue—severance of all connection between the body and the brain. Which is interesting, because the brain continues to function more or less normally . . . you can actually watch yourself behaving in this terrible way, but you can't control it."
—Hunter S. Thompson, *Fear and Loathing in Las Vegas*

Diethyl ether is used in biology labs as a solvent and an anesthetic.

CHUGGING COUGH SYRUP

In the '60s, kids started chugging cough syrup to get at the alcohol and codeine. Codeine cough medicine hasn't been available over the counter for years. But people are still chugging cough syrup. Why? Because it still contains alcohol and because the active ingredient these days is dextromethorpan or DM/DXM, which gets you high. Known as "Robo" or "Red Devil," DM is a key ingredient in nighttime cough medicines like Robitussin DM, Comtrex, Nyquil, Vicks 44D, Corcidin Cold and Cough pills, and Contac Cough Caps.

- **Advantage:** It's not considered addictive, maybe because it tastes so bad.
- **Disadvantage:** It's a short high with a long, rugged slide down afterward. It doesn't mix well with other substances and sometimes gives you "Robo itch."

HALLUCINOGENS

True country druggies don't bother with the street scene. They grow their own pot and know how to spot hallucinogenic psilocybin mushrooms, which grow naturally in cow shit. People may go out of their way to pick them, but hallucinogens are a plant's natural defense against deer, who see tripping as a bad thing. To each his own.

NUTMEG

Nutmeg has hallucinogenic effects because it contains myristicine, which is chemically similar to Ecstasy. "The Camel," a veteran tripper, has been eating powdered nutmeg since the 1970s and says you should "plan ahead for nutmeg because the effects last well over twenty-four hours."

- **Advantage:** It's legal and if taken in sufficient quantities, could produce a long-lasting, low-grade trip.
- **Disadvantage:** The dose required produces a severe hangover and stomach irritation, and an overdose will make you even sicker.

UP IN SMOKE

With high cigarette taxes and IDs required to buy even at Dixie Gas, some smokers are returning to cracker alternatives to tobacco, which flourished in the forties . . .

- **Advantage:** You can smoke under age and smoke for free.
- **Disadvantage:** No nicotine, and some of the weeds out there will make your tongue numb. All smoke increases your risk of getting lung cancer.

RABBIT TOBACCO

Rabbit tobacco refers to a few different kinds of wild weeds that grow in most fields and pastures of the South, but it's certainly not just *any* weed. Also known as "life everlasting" or "rabbit grass," all of these weeds (belladonna is one) contain the brain-altering compound atropine or an atropinelike substance, which gives you a high similar to that of pot, dry mouth and all.

Harvested and allowed to dry, rabbit tobacco is traditionally rolled in the brown paper from grocery bags. And in the forties, smoking it was a rite of passage for many country boys.

CORN SILK

"All one needed for a fine smoke with corn silk was the tassel or silk from ripe ears of corn, a brown paper sack, and matches. The corn silk must be dry and a deep purple, reddish color to be right for smoking. The silk was rolled into pieces of sack paper, making a nice long cigar."—Carolyn Bintin Eveland, *The Bluff, the Railroad and the Hobo*

Silksmokers seal the stogie with spit, and light it up so it flames. After blowing out the flame, the cornsilk stogie is ready to be puffed.

MUSCADINE VINES

Muscadine vines grow everywhere the kudzu hasn't gotten to and are a classic first smoke. Remove the veins from muscadine leaves. Soak the leaves for two days in saltwater. Cut them up and replace in saltwater for two more days. Dry in the sun. Smoke.

OTHER SMOKABLES

During the German occupation of France, tobacco was nowhere to be found, so most French smokers smoked coltsfoot, a weed still commonly used in herbal cigarettes.

Often used to flavor pipe tobacco, all these leaves can be smoked by themselves: magnolia flowers, clover blossoms, lavender petals, rose petals, walnut leaves, chestnut leaves, birch leaves, pear leaves, cherry leaves, fig leaves, rose leaves, tomato leaves, artichoke leaves, sage, verbena, and wormwood.

Wash and dry leaves. Let them dehydrate slowly in a dark place, or put them in a pillowcase and set out in the sun (or in the oven on warm or in the dryer on low).

FOR THE STONED

Now that pot has a higher street value than gold, stoners have found ways to grow their own without attracting attention. Actually, the biggest export crop in Kentucky is weed. Farmers plant it deep in the forests, leave, and don't come back until the harvest. A man near

Granite Falls, Oregon, once grew plants in an old school bus buried beneath his backyard. The entrance was hidden in a fake outhouse. (Get found out, go to p. 190.)

Growing aside, stoners have also found creative ways to smoke it:

Bongs: Aka water pipes, they clean and cool the smoke. They can be fashioned from almost anything: soda bottles, beer cans, vases, Mason jars, slop buckets, plastic honey bears, and milk jugs. And bongs have been filled with everything from icicles to bourbon.

Sports Needle One-Hitter: A sports needle (the thing you use to blow up a basketball) can also be used as a ready-made one-hitter: The smoke comes through the hollow needle, but the hole is small enough that the ashes don't.

LIQUOR (BEFORE BEER . . .)

The best country song has yet to be written—"Six-Pack Sucker on a Saturday Night." But for those who are under age, live in dry counties, are too cheap, or live too deep in the woods to bother going to town, liquor can be made at home.

HOME FERMENTATION

Fermentation is what happens when sugar and yeast meet. Yeast eats sugar and excretes alcohol, so it's easy to get started, and anyone who's forgotten a jug of cider in the back of the refrigerator knows it can happen all by itself. But alcohol made from air-fermented juice doesn't taste too good and is most often resorted to by prisoners, soldiers in the field, and teenagers who can't get a decent ID. For years, farmers have made dandelion wine, but it is a labor of love in the face of wine-in-a-box. And if you're into microbrew it might be worth making your own beer, but it's nowhere near as cheap and easy as picking up a case of PBR. In dry counties, bootleggers sell cases of beer in parking lots, and most people can get what they want without resorting to brewing it at home. But that's not to say moonshine is done for.

LOOK HERE

Don't miss the Annual Moonshiner's Reunion and Mountain Music Festival, held the first weekend in October at Woodstick Farm, near South Carolina's Dark Corners—prime moonshine country.

MOONSHINE

Moonshiners still distill homemade liquor from corn and wheat in the backwoods and can be vicious when someone encroaches on their territory. When park service worker Eric O'Conner arrived in a

Kentucky moonshine hotspot, the first thing the rangers told him was; "If you see those fires at night, stay away. The bootleggers will shoot you." And that was in the 1990s. (Go to p. 62.)

I've been a moonshiner for seventeen long years
I've spent all my money on whiskey and beer
I go to some hollow and set up my still
And if whiskey don't kill me then I don't know what will.
—TRADITIONAL APPALACHIAN FOLK SONG

To some, moonshine may smell like kerosene and rotten eggs, but to others, it's worth risking life and limb. Charley Weems, a retired ATF agent, spent most of his life chasing bootleggers and hunting for stills, but his biggest catch came in 1962, a still owned by a man known as "J.R." It was one of the largest stills Weems had ever seen with a 20-foot biler and 54 fermenters holding 220 gallons apiece. "There were 1,260 gallons of moonshine and 10,000 gallons of beer ready to be shipped. . . . Since the chicken house used to cover the still was subject to destruction as well as the still, and transporting that much equipment and product would be nearly impossible, we decided to blow up the entire operation. No sooner had I gotten behind a big oak tree than the explosives began going off. The roof lifted as several sticks of dynamite went off at

the same time. Amber beer came pouring out of the cracks. I had been concerned about fire, but with that much beer flying in all directions there was no chance of that" (Charlie Weems, *A Breed Apart*). (Go to p. 190.)

And when all the bootleggers have gone to bed and

you're feeling the need to celebrate, don't go reaching for the Champale. Consider this option first:

MOUNTAIN MAN CHAMPAGNE
10 gallons white wine, Rhine or Sauterne
3 pounds rock candy dissolved in 1½ pints water
½ gallon grain alcohol, 190 proof
⅛ tsp. citric acid
⅛ tsp. bicarbonate of soda (baking soda)

Mix the above ingredients together. Bottle the solution, cork, and store in a cool cellar. (Taken from *The Manual for the Manufacture of Cordials*, by Christian Schultz, 1862.)

DRINK YOUR BEER!

"I had this beer brewed up just for me. I think it's the best beer I've ever tasted, and I've tasted a lot. I think you'll like it too." —Billy Carter, on the Billy Beer can

PRESIDENTIAL BEER

Billy Carter, brother of the ex-president, introduced his beer in 1977 at six dollars a six-pack. But no one would drink it because it tasted too bad. Even when he reduced the price to ninety-nine cents a six-pack, it was a loser, and Billy claimed he was drunk when he picked out the flavor. But in 1980, a mysterious collector put out an ad claiming he wanted to buy Billy beer cans for $200 apiece, and the Billy Beer can scam began.

This advertiser created a false market, and hundreds of people shelled out big for a can that is now hardly worth fifty cents. Herb Schwartz, past president of the Beer Can Collectors of America, said,

"There is no evidence that the guy actually bought a can for two hundred dollars but we suspect he probably sold some." At the height of the Billy Beer scam there were as many as two hundred and twenty ads for Billy Beer cans.

Scandal aside, other democrats have used signature beer to their advantage. In the 1990s Billary beer was "the politically correct choice." Its label read: "Remember the solution to our nation's economic woes is in your hand," and David Kaufman, co-owner of Presidential Bottlers Inc.—manufacturer of the beer—claimed that it was made from "Bill barley and Hillary hops, with slightly tainted Whitewater water and Arkansas charm."

WAYS TO GET THE TOP OFF A BOTTLE OF BEER

"The crackers I hang out with pride themselves on being able to open beer bottles that don't have twist-off caps with various objects other than a proper bottle opener. . . . My claim to fame is opening a bottle with a dime."
—Cousin Hank, Fort Collins, Colorado

The big buck knife is also common, but the braggarts among us use spoons, screwdrivers, wrenches, lighters, countertop corners, or the corner of the bumper of a 1978 Ford pickup.

VIETNAM FUEL-COOLED BEER

One Vietnam vet claimed that during the war he and his pals would sometimes bury warm cans of beer in the dirt, cover the area with jet fuel, and set it on fire. According to them, when the fire went out, an endothermic reaction in the soil would cool the beer. Dangerous and dubious, yes. But so was the war. And with chugging, funneling, shotgunning, drinking games, and keg stands, there's more to beer than sipping off a can.

HIDE YOUR VICE

Since vices are generally looked down on, people have been as inventive about hiding them as doing them.

WHERE TO GET WASTED

- **Underage Cornfield Keggers:** A teenage classic in the corn-belt is to take kegs deep into a cornfield, then cut down a patch of corn, making a party space that's impossible to see from the road and impossible to find in the maze of corn without directions (sixteen rows in, take a right; at the irrigation arm, take a left; three rows down . . .). The hard part is finding your way out again, drunk.
- **Graveyards** are often used for the same thing. As long as it's not a famous graveyard, there are usually no night watchmen. And as long as it's big enough, no one will find you without directions (behind the Mercer crypt, third row of headstones on the right). The problem with this is that it sometimes flips people out when the ghosts come over and ask if they can do keg stands.
- **Golf Courses** serve the same function for the suburban set. (Directions: thirteenth hole, sandtrap, just below the green.) Problem: night sprinklers.

QUICK CLEAR-UPS

Once the damage is done, you won't be sober until you are sober, but you can try to look that way:

- **Visine** for bloodshot eyes.
- **Pickle juice** hides pot breath. Any die-hard household maven will tell you that vinegar removes odors, so that, combined

with a little essence of garlic, should throw the drug hounds off your scent.

- **Tomato juice** hides booze breath. (By the way, tomato juice also neutralizes skunk.) But remember, it works on the nose alone, not the breathalyzer. Speaking of which, you may have heard that putting pennies under your tongue will help you beat the test. Don't count on it, sweetheart.

- **Peppermint schnapps and vodka** smell freshest on your breath. Gin smells the worst.

BEAT THE SHAKES

And if it gets that bad, there is a bar towel trick that, according to Lewis Nordan, will help you get a drink to your mouth when your hands are shaking from the DTs: "You drape the towel around your neck, holding it by either end with your hands. You pull the towel down slowly across the back of your neck toward the table with one hand—this stabilizes your hands so you can grasp the shot glass—and then you pull slowly and firmly on the towel with the other hand so that it draws the hand with the drink in it steadily up to your mouth. The first shot of vodka rises slowly to your face and no matter how shaky your hands, the drink is controlled and stabilized by the towel. You don't spill a drop" (Lewis Nordan, *Boy with Loaded Gun*).

PASSING A DRUG TEST

"I never had a problem with drugs, only with the cops."—Keith Richards

Modern science has proven that the only creatures likely to survive a nuclear fallout are the cockroaches and Keith Richards. Over the years, the aging pop star has become a poster child for sustained drug abuse, managing to stay on his feet and feed his habit for almost four decades. Even if you're as hardy as Keith, he probably never had to succumb to a drug test. And you might as well face it, there's not all that much you can do to hide the drugs in your piss. But that doesn't mean people haven't tried. Here's how:

- **Dog Piss:** No dice. Under a microscope, animal urine looks completely different from a human's.
- **Ibuprofen:** Take a bunch and blame it on that. This used to work. About ten years ago, there was evidence that people who had just taken ibuprofen could "trigger a positive test for marijuana," but the new the tests are more advanced, and this won't happen anymore.
- **Contact High:** Saying you got a contact high won't work. Test centers claim that they've put "clean" people in rooms filled with pot smoke for hours on end and they still test negative for drugs.
- **Codeine Cough Medicine:** Saying you took codeine cough medicine may work, because it does test positive in drug tests. But they'll probably ask for your prescription or make you take the test again later.
- **Poppy Seeds:** Once upon a time, there was a chance that eating poppy seeds could increase your risk of flunking a drug test, but these days, poppy seeds are required to have such low opiate levels that even eating bags of them will leave no trace on the tests.
- **Cleansers:** Vinegar, Goldenseal, and detox teas sometimes work to dilute the urine to a point where drugs cannot be detected, but they're not very reliable. You might slide by, but even so, your suspiciously watery urine will probably just buy you a retest.
- **Blood:** Putting a drop of blood in the urine can make things awfully confusing for lab technicians. The blood cell molecules can sometimes absorb the drug molecules, but blood is just not supposed to be there. If you are a woman, you can claim that

you're on the rag. If you're a man, maybe you got punched in the kidneys in the bar last night. Either way you're probably looking at take two.

- **FYI:** Lab technicians have reported finding traces of Drano, lemon juice, Visine, WD-40, salt, and Clorox added to urine to try to throw the test. No dice.
- Your best bet is to sneak in someone else's urine. Someone clean.

DUDS

Rumors of euphoric dreams, waiting for you in the most unlikely places, have been circulating for years. But most of them don't work.

Coca-Cola and Aspirin Will Not Lead You to Chemical Nirvana: The rumor runs that a mixture of Coca-Cola and aspirin is an aphrodisiac, a great way to get high, and sometimes causes instant death. This is purest B.S.

Banana Peels Are Not Mellow: Countless bored teenagers have tried toasting the threads of bananas and smoking them. *The Anarchist Cookbook* even went so far as to call it "bananadine." But it doesn't work. People picked it up from the "electrical banana" line in Donovan's song "Mellow Yellow" and then turned it around. They started the rumor that Donovan wrote the song in order to extol the virtues of a little-known drug made from banana peels. But Donovan was more likely singing about how he felt on LSD. As for bananas, you might as well go out and smoke corn silk.

Marjoram: Don't Be Duped: Marjoram may look, smell, and even taste a bit like pot, but it is in the oregano family and is in no way related to cannabis.

No Glory: People say you can trip off eating morning glory seeds, and in certain places it's true. Some morning glory seeds contain a chemical very similar to LSD, but the seeds of the morning glory native to the United States are not hallucinogenic.

Poppycock: There are reports of people who have gotten giddy on poppy-head tea, but then there are also folks who believe in sprites, dancing cars, and gnomes.

Prison

"What we've got here is failure to communicate." —PRISON CHAIN GANG CAPTAIN, *Cool Hand Luke*

A **mushfake** is anything made by a prisoner, and they're good at it: "Not only the worst of the young are sent to prison, but the best, that is, the proudest, the bravest, the most daring, the most enterprising of the poor" (Norman Mailer, from the introduction to Jack Henry Abbot's *In the Belly of the Beast*).

Old Sparky: Old Sparky, an electric chair that fried 361 men between 1924 and 1964, was handmade by some incarcerated craftsmen. It was built sturdily enough to outlive all its occupants and a stint in the prison dump. Old Sparky was recovered and donated to the Texas Prison Museum.

GUEST BOOK

1. Clyde Barrow
2. David Allen Coe
3. _____
4. _____
5. _____
6. _____
7. _____

HOMEMADE PRISON WEAPONS

Shivs/Shanks/Gats/Bangers/Burners/ Blades: Homemade knives are fashioned from any object that can be sharpened on the cement prison floor.

Lock in Sock: Combination lock in a sock used to club people.

TATTOOS/TATS/TACS/INKS

JAILHOUSE TATTOO GUN

"For the needle a guitar string or paper clip is sharpened to a fine point on a rock or contraband sandpaper, or the side of the metal sink. It is run through the hollow shaft of a ballpoint pen and the tip protrudes slightly from the writing end. At the upper end, the string is attached to a small motor, usually from a Walkman, and hooked up to batteries. The apparatus is fortified for stability by being taped to popsicle sticks or a plastic eating utensil. The pen remains stable while the point jumps."—PHYLLIS KORNFIELD, *Cell Block Visions*

Prison ink can be made from black pen ink, scrapings from soft pastels, charcoal pencils, burned black chess pieces, carbon paper, a mixture of molten rubber and sugar, or a combination of toothpaste, shampoo, water, and smoke from a burnt razor blade. Or some people burn the pages of a book. Lightweight pages like those from the Bible work best. They collect up the soot and mix with toothpaste and water.

TATTOO REMOVAL

"In desperation, people remove tattoos by burning them off with a cigarette or pouring acid on them."
—JOSH KORMAN,
Western Journal of Medicine

Country

"If that ain't country, I'll kiss your ass."

—David Allen Coe

THE FAT OF THE LAND

DOWN ON THE FARM

"She thinks my tractor's sexy."
—Kenny Chesney

Hundreds of things are jerry-rigged on small farms every day. Farmers use baling wire to keep tractors running and to lock barn doors. They protect lightning-struck trees by covering the wound with aluminum siding. They flood barns to out the rats. On-hand ingenuity is part of the daily routine on the unmechanized farm, and hats off to them all, but we reserved this section for the truly inspired.

VIRTUAL CATTLE GUARDS

Painted cattle guards are cheaper to make than real ones: Just paint black and white stripes across the road. These painted guards are almost as common as the real ones out West, and they actually work. The cattle think the black stripes are holes in the ground and won't walk across the paint job. Some say it works because cows are color blind. Others say it's because they lack depth perception. Or maybe cows are just stupid.

THE GOAT YOKE

An Alabama goat keeper made this invention to keep his cleverest goat from crawling over, under, or though his electric fence. (It also works on sheep and cows.) Take a wide leather collar and attach four stiff wires to the collar so the wire juts out in four directions like four long spikes. Put the spiked collar on the goat so when he sticks his head between the electric wires, one of the four spikes will contact the electric wire and zap him.

CHICKEN COOP ALARM CLOCK

It's a known fact among chicken farmers that hens lay more eggs when there is more light, so one New Hampshire farmer used to get up to turn the lights on in the henhouse before dawn to make the chickens think it was already morning. But he got tired of losing sleep, so this is what he did:

He tied one end of a piece of string to the light switch. He tied the other end to a small rock just heavy enough to flip the switch. He balanced the rock on a wind-up alarm clock and set the alarm for the time he wanted the light to go on. When the alarm went off, the unwinding alarm mechanism would make the clock vibrate, and the vibrations would knock the rock off. The rock's fall would pull the light switch on, so the hens would get up but the farmer could sleep in.

SHOE FERTILIZER

Old leather shoes can be used for more than door stops and homes for little old women. "Grapevines need a slow fertilizer because they quit bearing if heavily nitrogenized. Shoes, being leather, were rich in nitrogen and since they decomposed gradually the fertilizer would slowly enter the ground." (Janisse Ray, *Ecology of a Cracker Childhood*)

TRUCK-HULLED WALNUTS

Black walnuts are considered one of the best-tasting nuts in the world, but you never see them in supermarkets. Why? Because they are encased in a tough green hull, and their shells are very, very hard. . . . But in Jackson County, Kentucky, people have found you can hull black walnuts quite easily. Spread them out in the driveway and drive over them repeatedly with a pickup truck. The hulls will break off but the nutshells will stay intact.

DETONATING ANIMAL CORPSES TO STAVE OFF BEARS

Keeping bears away from livestock in rural areas can be a chore when the animals are alive, but nothing attracts bears like a dead pony or cow. Farmers bury their dead animals, unless it's impossible to get them in the ground because it's frozen or full of rocks. When this is the case (if you are squeamish, stop reading here), farmers drag the dead animal out of the way and stuff dynamite into its throat and intestines. When they light the fuse, the animal explodes, scattering meat everywhere. The meat quickly dries out, and the bears have nothing to come after.

LAZY MULES

For hundreds of years, farmers have used mules to turn stiles to generate energy. The mule walks around and around, turning gears that grind corn, power churns, or whatever else. This works as long as the mule keeps moving. But the mule doesn't want to keep moving. The mule wants to chill in the shade and watch you turn the stile. You can stand there and "encourage" him to keep going, but it becomes a real problem when you actually need to be elsewhere to use the mule-power; as soon as you leave, he stops in the shade.

Since the carrot-on-a-stick thing doesn't really work, keeping the mule moving in this case takes some extra imagination. Potter Jerry Brown recorded himself swearing "move it" oaths at his mule for an hour. Then he tied a tape recorder to the mule's harness and played back the tape while he was inside, quietly working on the mule-powered pottery wheel. The mule never stopped until that tape ran out. George Washington Daugherty, a chair maker in Larue County, Kentucky, cut a window in the wall above his lathe and used a slingshot to pop the mule in the rump with a piece of gravel whenever it tried to stop.

ENGINE HORSEPOWER

Many small-time farm operations have consolidated, and mules have been replaced by large, electrically powered machines. But some have stuck it out with the stiles, if not the mules. They rig their stiles up to old truck engines instead. Automobile engines are also used to power circular saws. In fact, the first rope-tow on a ski mountain was powered by an old model-A engine.

PIG-SHIT POWER

"It might surprise a lot of people, but manure can be nearly odor-free."
—Paul Miller, USDA Natural Resources Conservation Service

All animal manure gives off methane, but fermented swine shit gives off the most: The methane generated by the manure fermentation of five pigs is enough to cook three hot meals each day for an average family.

To transform pig shit into energy, you need a digester. It looks like a small water tower and is full of manure. The manure naturally contains bacteria that digests it anaerobically (without air) to produce methane. The digester is sealed with a cover that traps the methane and pumps it out into a holding tank. From there, you can use it like natural gas. Once all the methane is digested out, the remaining manure can be used as fertilizer.

The USDA Natural Resources Conservation Service has already built many successful digesters for farmers in Iowa. But if you're not on the list, you can make a simple one of your own. Lay out 50 feet of 36-inch culvert pipe. Feed manure into one end and collect fertilizer from the other, sealing each end while not in use. In the middle of the pipe drill a hole for the methane. Fit a pipe from there to a holding tank and you're all set. One problem with the digester is cold weather. Bacteria thrive in temperatures close to the body temperature of the pig, so if you want to run your digester during cold weather, you may find that it takes more energy than it gives off to keep the system warm enough.

THE AMERICAN HICK RIFLE

During the frontier days, hunters in the wilds of Western Pennsylvania wanted a gun with long-range accuracy for hunting coons and rabbits, so they rebuilt their German rifle-barreled guns, adding an extremely long homemade barrel. During the revolution, the Boston minutemen laughed at the long-barreled rifles when the strangely dressed Pennsylvanians arrived. But they stopped laughing after the first shots were fired. The Pennsylvania "hicks" repeatedly hit 7-inch target posts from 250 yards. Using their standard smooth-bore muskets, the minutemen's best shooters couldn't hit the same target from 100 yards. The British so came to dread the coon hunters and their guns that George Washington had other troops disguise themselves as the Pennsylvanians to scare off British troops.

HUNTING

"Shooting street signs drunk out of a pickup truck greatly increases your shot-to-kill ratio during whitetail deer season!"—Russell Davenport

For some, nothing clears the head like packing out into the great outdoors. For others, nothing clears the head like packing out into the great outdoors with a gun and coming back with a deer strapped to the back of the Chevy.

DEER

Deer are timid, so hunting them requires patience. A deer stand or blind gives hunters a place to hide and a place to sit while they wait for the deer all day long.

Truck-Body Deer Stand: You can build a convenient deer stand by hoisting an old car or truck body up onto rebar stilts and welding it into place. (Gut the engine, transmission, radiator, etc., to make it much lighter.) *Advantage:* Ready-made, waterproof, bear proof, and comes with comfy deluxe seats. If you spend the night, you can use the truck bed to sleep on and even make your fire.

Hide Your Scent: You need to hide your human scent to get anywhere near a truly wild animal, and hanging a Christmas tree car deodorizer around your neck won't work. Before the hunt, let your breakfast fire burn down and put a pile of fresh-cut green pine branches and needles on the coals. When they start to smoke, jump through the smoke three or four times in your hunting clothes. The pine sap will coat you with a thin layer of residue, which should feel slightly sticky until it dries. Finally, give your boots an extra coat by holding your feet in the smoke. You will be piney fresh all day.

"A deer should have enough brains to tan its own hide."
—Old Tanning Axiom

After the Kill: You can skin your deer with a golf ball (see page 211) and bring the meat and the hide home.

How to Tan a Deer Hide Using a Washing Machine: Carefully scrape the fat and hair off the deer hide. Cook the deer's brains in a pot, stirring them with a wooden spoon until they get soupy. (If you feel the need for extra brains, you can add some beef brains from the butcher shop.) If you're a traditionalist, you can put brains and deer-skin in a tub and leave them for a few days, stirring occasionally. The tannic acid in the deer brain will tan your hide. Or forget the tub and stick the hide and brains in the washing machine. Two "color" cycles should do it.

"I know a guy, who mechanized and sped up this part of the process. He put the whole mess in his Maytag washer and ran it. He did get a divorce later but I'm not sure if that was the reason." —Rick M., folklorist, Madison, Wisconsin

FYI: Watch Your Brain: A morbid note on traditions involving animal brains, including the backwoods Kentucky custom of offering guests squirrel brains: You could catch Creutzfeld-Jakob disease, the fatal human form of "mad cow."

TURKEY

"I've had to shoot at turkeys in more weird positions than you could find in the Kama Sutra." —Jay L., veteran hunter and National Wild Turkey Federation member

Camp Cooking

HOBO STOVE: If you want to cook out without an expensive camp stove, make your own. Take a gallon paint can and clean out all the paint. Punch holes around the top rim and larger holes around the bottom. Start a fire, and turn the can down, bottom side up, over the flames. The wind will blow through the bottom holes and feed the fire. Exhaust will come through the holes at the top of the can. The bottom of the can is your built-in hot plate.

HOT HOBO BREAKFAST: Coat the inside of a tuna can with vegetable oil. Crack an egg into the can, add a couple Little Smokies, and cover with foil. Place can on a hobo stove until the egg is cooked. Eat on a biscuit with a slice of cheese.

HOT FOOD FOR THE EXTREMELY LAZY: Want a hot dog without bothering with the fire? Some opt for the mini propane torch method, which works as long as you keep the flame moving over the dog. Or you can also rely on the sun and a can of Pringles. Eat the Pringles. Cut horizontal slits at each end of tube, then cut a long vertical slit to connect them, so the slits look like a capital "i". Fold back the cut sections to be your solar reflectors. Push a skewer through the middle of the bottom of the tube, then skewer your hot dog. Replace the Pringles cap, and skewer that too, so the dog is suspended inside the tube. Put the tube out in the sun, fiddle with your solar panels to focus as much sun on the dog as possible, and wait for it to cook.

TURKEY IN A GARBAGE CAN: Heat a bunch of charcoal briquets in a fire pit. Push a thick wooden stick (sharpened at both ends) into the ground. Then impale a turkey on the stake, making sure it holds solid. Pour a can of Mr. Pibb over the turkey for flavor. Put a layer of hot coals around the stake. Hang a metal bucket over the turkey, so the rim is a couple of inches off the ground. Put a ring of coals around the rim, and pile coals on top of the bucket. Finally, put a large metal garbage can over the whole rig. Prop up one side of the can with a rock to let in some air. A medium turkey will take a couple of hours to cook.

Don't Be a Turkey: "Statistically, turkey hunting is four times safer than Ping-Pong, and you are fifty times more likely to take a trip to the emergency room if you play golf," says Rob K. of the National Wild Turkey Federation. But to keep those odds, you must never wear red, white, or blue, because another hunter is likely to mistake you for a turkey and shoot you. And never wave to alert another hunter of your presence—the trigger-happy are likely to shoot at the movement—so you should yell instead. (Go to p. 62.)

Bulletproof Tree Blind: A large tree trunk is the best kind of blind for hunting turkeys, because you can pivot around the tree to track a circling bird and because you can sit up against it (necessary back support after all those *Kama Sutra* positions). Best of all, you'll also have a bulletproof barrier between yourself and another overexcited hunter.

Taxidermy Tips—a Turkey in Tights: To take your turkey to the taxidermist without messing up the feathers, cut both legs off a pair of panty hose, and throw out the panties. Then, cut about two feet off of the top of each leg (the thigh area). Knot up one end and leave the other end free. Each of these will carry a big turkey. If you are into smaller birds, like duck, for instance, you'll need to use the bottom of the hose legs (the calf area). Slide the dead bird headfirst into the stocking, and then knot the open end. The feathers will all be held in place, flat against the bird's body, and when the taxidermist receives your catch, all he has to do is cut open the head end of the stocking and pull out the bird.

WILD BOAR

"The pig didn't know I was there. It's my kick. I love shafting animals. It's rock 'n' roll power."—Ted Nugent

If you want your wild boar alive, set a trap and put out some hog bait to lure the animal over. Many of these traps are quite basic (i.e., an empty pen with the gate left open). If you want your hog dead, take your dogs out into the woods, track one down, and shoot it. If you're really lazy, you let it get caught in the trap first, and then shoot it. Simple, but that's not real feral swine hunting . . . there are all kinds of ways to raise the stakes in this sport:

Feral Swine Hunting: If you've ever seen a dude wrestle a 350-pound hog to the ground you'll understand why this is considered to be an extreme sport. For extreme feral swine hunting, you'll need some hunting hounds and a rope. Have the dogs detain the boar while you rush in, grab the boar by its hind leg, snatch a fistful of its back-hair, and yank it up off the ground. Using your knee as a battering ram, slam the boar into the ground. Then leap on top of the boar, jam your knee into its neck, grab the hind legs, and tie them to one of the front legs. If, by this time you haven't been gored, bitten, or crushed, you can assume your boar is hobbled.

Extreme Feral Swine Hunting: No dogs. This is all about you trying to kill a 350-pound boar with a spear.

Ultra-Extreme Feral Swine Hunting: Same as above, substituting a bowie knife for the spear.

And here's what Donna D., a fine Texas hog-hunting woman, had to say at the end of her hunt: "I was a good girl, I had a great time and I brought home the bacon. So there."

Hog Bait

Mix corn with water in a bucket and let it sit for a few days. You can mix in some Jell-O for a sweet bait or beer for a sour bait. Some people slop in a little diesel fuel to deter other animals from eating it, because the hogs don't care. They'll eat anything: As far as they're concerned the corn's at its sexiest when it's completely rancid.

FISHING

Fishing is sometimes known as drowning worms, but only if you don't catch any fish. The key is often the right kind of bait or lure, which, for the thrifty, doesn't have to come from a store.

BAIT

- **Worm Grunting** (also known as "twiddling") is still the best way to get worms out of the ground for bait. The enterprising grunter saves himself the trouble of digging for worms by rubbing a piece of iron and a chunk of hickory wood (known as a "stob") together on the ground, causing vibrations that make the worms freak out. They rush to the earth's surface, where they are easily scooped up.
- **Rubber Bands:** You can use a rubber band instead of a worm, and bucketmouth bass won't notice the difference until it's too late. Number 84 rubber bands are the kind to use (about one-half inch thick, three inches long). Cut a #84 in half, making two long, straight strips to be used for two separate lures. Tie

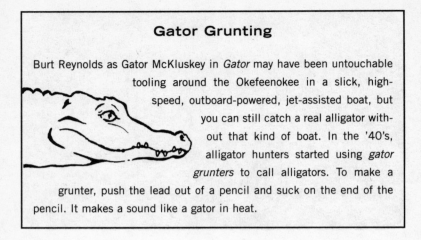

Gator Grunting

Burt Reynolds as Gator McKluskey in *Gator* may have been untouchable tooling around the Okefeenokee in a slick, high-speed, outboard-powered, jet-assisted boat, but you can still catch a real alligator without that kind of boat. In the '40's, alligator hunters started using *gator grunters* to call alligators. To make a grunter, push the lead out of a pencil and suck on the end of the pencil. It makes a sound like a gator in heat.

one end of the rubber band piece to the hook and then make a cut to split the bottom end of the piece so the two little bits wiggle back and forth with the current to convince the fish it's alive.

- **WD-40:** An old-timer in the Midwest challenged a local outdoor writer to a fishing contest, boasting that he could outfish the writer two-to-one with his secret weapon. He did it, and the writer spilled the secret: spraying the bait with WD-40. Now there's hardly a salmon- or bass-fishing boat in the water that doesn't carry a can (except those who swear by PAM cooking spray, instead).
- **Wheaties and Big Red:** Carp have a sweet tooth. To catch them, crush Wheaties and mix in some Big Red soda. Keep mashing it until it turns into a dough that you can form into balls and put on a hook.
- **Barbie Locks:** Russian fishermen in the northern Pacific discovered that Barbie's golden hair worked really well in attracting fish. Quickly adopted by fishermen in the United States, Barbie's been spending a lot of time underwater lately.

- **True Spoons:** You might think spoon fishing-lures are called "spoons" because they look like real spoons, but, really, spoon lures look like real spoons because they're trying to look like lures, which really *are* spoons. . . . Take an old tablespoon and cut off the handle with wire cutters. Drill a small hole at each end of the curved part of the spoon. Put a thin wire ring through each hole. Attach the narrow end to the hook and the wider end to the line. You can also paint one side with red nail polish. The inner curved part of the spoon makes the lure wiggle in the water, and the silver makes it shine like a minnow.

FISHING WITHOUT A POLE

"Morning, the biggest, splashing down middle of the creek, with the others carrying jars and sacs of twenty-penny nails, and fastening a piece of bacon to the bottom of every knee-deep pool they came to. By the time they got back to where they'd started, there'd be frantic invasions of crawdads, all milling around unable to get the bacon loose. Procedure then was to bring out a minnow bag on a stick, hit the crawdad on the nose with the stick, and catch it, as it jumped, in the bag." —Thomas Pynchon, *Vineland*

- **Cooning:** Bears can slap salmon out of rushing rivers, but even the quickest, strongest mountain man might find that beyond his reach. The raccoon has overcome his size disadvantage with a method human hands can also master: Find a place in the slow-moving shallows of river that is thick with roots and plants. Hide your hands in the roots and wait for a fish. When one comes along, slap it hard up onto the bank.
- **Old-Style Found-Object Fishing:** Nineteenth-century trappers would fish with a hook made from a bent safety pin and a line made of horsehair.

Idiot Box: Flying Fish

One summer night, in Montana, even though it was pitch black out, Mr. Stout and his buddy decided to go fishing. When a bass nabbed Mr. Stout's top-water lure, he set the hook too hard, jerking the fish out of the water so that it came hurtling toward the boat. But it was dark out there, and Mr. Stout didn't realize that the airborne fish was heading straight for his face . . . the treble hook caught him in the nose, and he stumbled around in the boat with the fish dangling from his nostril. Mr. Stout's buddy unhooked the fish (which he tossed back in the water because it wasn't that big anyway) and then extracted the lure from Mr. Stout's nose. Luckily for Mr. Stout, he was left only with a small scar.

- **Contemporary Found-Object Fishing:** A good twentieth-century Boy Scout knows how to make a survival fishing kit: Tie one end of a length of fishing line to a thread spool and the other to a fishhook. When not in use, wrap the fishing line around the spool and carry the whole outfit in a 35mm film canister. When it comes time to fish, un-spool the line, hold onto the spool end, and snap the film canister near the hook to use as a bobber.

FISH FOR DINNER

- **Bottle-Top Scaler:** Make a primitive scaler by nailing metal bottle tops to a block of wood. For best results scrape against the direction of the fish's scales.
- **Dishwasher Fish:** You may fish with your bare hands, but there's no reason to keep it primitive when you get home. Wrap your fish up in foil, put it on the top shelf of your dish rack, and get your

washer running. Hot, of course, and no soap. A medium-sized mullet (fish, not hairstyle) should be ready after one regular cycle.

- **FYI: Smell Fishy?** If your hands smell fishy after cleaning a fish, cut a lemon slice and rub it over your hands before washing them.

BOATS

It's bad luck to change your boat's name. If you whistle it will bring up the wind, and you should always use your right foot first when embarking/disembarking from a boat. Strict rules, but anything that floats can be a boat.

Skimming on a Kitchen Table: Take your typical (sturdy) wooden kitchen table. Flip it over, and attach your outboard to one end. Put it in the water, jump in back by the motor, and get going. The weight of you plus the motor at the back of the table will cause the "nose" end to rise out of the water and you'll fly. Does not work with passengers. Just be careful whose table you take—Betty Cracker would NOT be happy.

Renaissance Man

Butch Anthony of 41 Poorhouse Road in Seale, Alabama, has taken country cracker ingenuity to such a level that we dedicate this section to him. To date, he has made well over a thousand inventions. These are but a few:

FARMING

Pot-Bellied-Pig-Powered Plow

"A rolling cage for pig-powered plowing. Cage is pulled two times weekly forward so pig can root up the ground and fertilize at the same time."
—Butch Anthony, January 1996

This is a movable pig house/pigpen. The house is a small tin shed with a flap door in the side for water and feed. The pigpen is attached to the front of the house. The sides are made of hog wire and two-by-fours; the bottom is open to the ground. At the front of the pigpen is a hitch that will hook to a tractor or a mule. The whole rig sits on wide iron wheels about a foot off the ground. The idea is for the pig to root around, turning the soil, and shit, fertilizing it. Every few days, you hitch up the mule and pull the pen forward a few yards. Eventually your field will be completely aerated and fertilized by the pig.

The Eggliminator: To catch a chicken snake, you'll need a steel trap from the hardware store, a stick of wax, and a medium-sized egg. Drip wax into the pan of the trap, and put egg in the wax. When the wax hardens, the egg won't move. "Put in chicken coop nest box. Snake tries to swallow egg and sets off trap around its head. Dead snake." (Butch Anthony, 1985)

HUNTING

Combination Deer Stand and Wheelbarrow: Make a ladder out of sturdy one-inch plastic tubing, and mount a makeshift canvas sling-seat on the top rung.

Bend the tops of the tubing out, and mount two bicycle wheels extending beyond the seat in both directions (so they spin). Lean the ladder up against a tree, with the wheel/seat part at the top, "wheels on each side of tree. Then when you kill a deer, rope it on and wheel it out." You can also mount a rack on the underside of the stand to hold your gun. (Butch Anthony, 1980)

Skinning a Deer with a Golf Ball: Lay the deer belly up. With a Bowie knife, cut a circle around the deer's genital area, then split hide from tail to throat. (Don't make the cut too deep; you don't want to pierce the stomach.) Cut from the split down each leg. Cut all the way around the neck and all four ankles, so the hide will peel off smoothly.

Take a golf ball and push it up under the tail part of the hide. Hang the deer from a tree by its hind legs. Tie a nylon rope around the ball and then hook the other end of the rope to the hitch of a pickup truck. "Loop three loops around the ball inside the hide and hook it to a pickup and drive forward slowly. Deer hide peels right off." (Butch Anthony, Winter 1977)

FISHING AND FROGGING

The Plop Fiz (Lure): The Plop Fiz is a hand-carved, wooden, fish-shaped lure with an eye-screw on the nose for the line. It's about five inches long and should be painted green with black and yellow spots, and red glass beads for eyes. Treble hooks are attached to either side of the fish's head, and one comes out of the tail. In its belly there is a hollow compartment that has a little screwed-on tin door with holes punctured in it. One of the screws is removable so you can twist the door open. "Add Alka Seltzer to compartment when finished with the lure. It bubbles and leaves a fizz trail which attracts fish." (Butch Anthony, July 2001)

The Period (Lure): This lure is the same as the Plop Fiz. What's different here is that the lure's midsection is a two-inch wire mesh compartment attached to the head and tail ends by screws. The screws at the tail end are removable, so you can put a bloody piece of bait into the mesh compartment. "This lure is designed to bleed and leave a blood trail. By adding blood bait to the wire mesh part, the fish-shaped lure bleeds when worked through the water." (Butch Anthony, July 2001)

Hypnotizing Frog Gig: Take a pitchfork (also known as a "frog gig"). Duct-tape a flashlight to the top of the handle so that it shines toward the tines. Glue a ball bearing to about a foot of fishing line and attach the line to one of the tines so the bearing can swing freely. Turn on the light and go find a frog. "The swinging of the ball bearing in the light of the flashlight looks like an insect in the moonlight to a frog. Puts him in a trance on the insect." And then he's easy to catch. (Butch Anthony, 1985)

Frog Harness (Lure): Make a frog head out of a cork so that your frog floats. Paint the cork green and add red glass eyes. Drive a five- to six-inch piece of electric fence wire straight though the center of the cork. Make a little wire loop on each end of that wire. (At the head end you will attach your fishing line, and at the rear end you will attach a double hook.) About an inch down from the head, attach another, shorter length of wire (about two inches) so that the whole contraption now looks like a cross made of wire with a cork on top. Attach a double hook on the end of each arm of the cross. The frog "harness" is really some lengths of thin copper wire. You basically crucify a live frog by putting his back up against the lure and wrapping the thin copper wire around each of his wrists to hold him securely to the two hooks up near the head, leaving both legs free. "Cast lure out in lake and frog's legs kicking attracts fish. Keeps bait alive longer". (Butch Anthony, July 2001)

AND DON'T FORGET . . .

The Happy Hooker (Carpenter's Helper): One of Butch's favorite inventions, the Happy Hooker is a simple hook you can screw temporarily into the wall to hold up the end of tape measure if you are working alone. Fine. But we think he likes it for his marketing campaign. "Hooks to hold the end of a tape measure. Tension at point of the screw holds tape measure end when you don't have helper to hold it for you." (Butch Anthony, 1998)

Car-Hood Rafts: Old-model car hoods that have a good curve work best. Strap inner-tubes to the underside of the hood, then flip and float. If you're feeling fancy, weld a few hubcaps to the top of the hood—concave-side up—to use as seats.

Keeping Business Afloat: During the Iowa floods of 1994, Lon Magyar's small business in Davenport was severely flooded. He hauled merchandise to dry land using a Huck Finn–style raft made from two canoes and three sheets of plywood.

Duck-Decoy Donut Boat: In the fifties, Robert Bogle, a waterfowl hunter, invented a boat that is a decoy in and of itself. Hoping to attract waterfowl from all directions, he put a carved duck on each corner of a very flat boat. Then, he made a man-sized hole in the middle and climbed into it up to his waist. Clad in rubber long johns, he propelled himself silently through the water toward his prey.

Arnold Hite takes a 200-mile drive upriver from Charleston, South Carolina, to the Food Lion Auto Fair in Concord, North Carolina. (Photo courtesy of www.bradbowling.com)

Amphicar: The Amphicar convertible, produced from 1961 to 1968, is the only nonmilitary vehicle of this kind ever to have gone into commercial production. With a maximum speed of 7 mph in water and 70 mph on land, it's not likely to win any races, but at least you can shake up your opponent by gliding into the drink. The car has twin nylon boat propellers and very high rear fins to prevent water from slopping in.

Photo courtesy of www.bradbowling.com

Cardboard Boats: The World Championship Cardboard boat race is held every July at Greers Ferry Lake, where recreational boat makers build their crafts out of cardboard, duct tape, glue, and paint. Chronically leaky and powered only by humans, these boats usually sink before they reach the finish line, and the most impressive sink wins the Titanic Award.

Stumpjumper: Serious boaters design their craft for a specific lake, and different styles of boats are typical for different lakes, depending on their geography. Dale Calhoun's lake, Reelfoot, in northern Tennessee, is full of stumps. His boat, *Stumpjumper,* is pointed at both ends, like a canoe, so it can slide over submerged logs. He also installed a reverse-oar mechanism so he can row in the direction he's facing, and thus see where he's going and avoid the stumps. The reverse-oar mechanism was passed down to him from his father and grandfather, who got it from a "guy named Allen," who patented it in the 1880s.

LOGGING WITH MUSCLES

Elijah "Tiger" White was a logger in Maine. In 1947 he and his team were felling pine above Richardson Lake, using crawler tractors to haul out the trees. But the terrain was so bare and rocky, the tractors would bump and bounce around, losing logs and jarring the logger's nerves. Finally Tiger got sick of it. "I'm not going to bounce over them rocks anymore." He said, "I won't see you for awhile, but I'll bring back something that'll ride a lot easier." Tiger came back a few weeks later with a four-wheel-drive snow plow he had named "Muscles" and had converted to hold logs. Muscles could haul three times as much as the crawler tractor, and the rubber tires made the ride out a lot easier. Muscles became known as a "skidder," and few years later the first commercial copy was built. Loggers still use skidders today.

SURVIVAL

Remember, when all the corn is gone, don't think there's nothing left to eat. . . . People used to eat cattail roots, and you can, too. Fresh out of toilet paper? No worries; cantaloupe leaves are big, fuzzy, and softer than Charmin'. Fierce survival instincts kept our ancestry around long enough to procreate, and if you're this deep in the woods, you can be sure you're "off the grid," so you'll need your own power.

WATER POWER

"One fellow in Cashton, Wisconsin, has a very small rivulet of a creek running through his farmstead less than ten yards from his house. He has a gatelike device that the flowing water swings back and forth steadily. It is attached to a wire that runs into a basement window. The wire makes a constant push-pull motion with a range of about one-and-a-half inches.
He said it runs a little generator that powers a freezer in the house.
He didn't invite me in to see it, however.
I asked him if using electricity to run something wasn't against his religion. He replied that it wasn't the electricity per se that was a problem. It was being hooked up into the utility network. Just about then, a delivery guy from the oil company pulled in to fill his fuel tank."

—Rick M., Madison, Wisconsin

WIND POWER

Windmills convert kinetic energy from the wind into energy we can use to generate electricity or pump water. Vollis Simpson, a folk inventor, built his first windmill to power his washing machine while he was stationed in Saipan during World War II. After returning to North Carolina, Simpson continued to experiment with wind power and whirligigs, eventually building a windmill large enough and powerful enough to heat his house. He builds most of his whirligigs from junk and found objects: scaffolding, bicycle wheels, highway reflectors, model airplanes, multiple propellers, gigantic poles, and street signs.

Corn Stove: In 1969, Carroll Buckner of Arden, North Carolina, invented a special stove for burning corn. And while he was president, Jimmy Carter kept one going in the Oval Office. You can pour fifty pounds of corn into the stove's hopper, light the fire, and walk away. The corn will burn for at least twenty-four hours, and you don't have to watch it or stoke it. It burns hotter and cleaner than wood, and unless you have your own woodlot, feed-corn bought down at the Seed & Feed is cheaper than wood, too. Judith Monroe of *Backwoods Home Magazine* says of her own corn habit, "It takes 2.2 bushels of corn to produce 1 million BTUs of heat, at an average cost of $8.79. Producing that much heat by burning wood costs, on average, $22.07." It's also kinder to the environment: Corn grows back in a few months; trees don't.

PIGGY NIGHT-LIGHT

Put a piece of hog lard in a saucer, light it on fire. It will burn brightly for an hour or so.

PORK FAT SOAP
4 gallons water
12 lbs. pork fat
2 cups coarse salt

Boil 3 gallons of water and fat for 2 hours. Add salt. Stir, bring back to boil, and let it bubble for a few minutes. Remove from stove. Add remaining gallon of water; stir slowly (add dried rosemary, mint, sage, or lemon peel to make it smell good). Let cool, cut into bars, and you've got soap.

WHISKEY-BOTTLE DRINKING GLASSES

Soak a piece of twine in coal oil, then tie it tightly around the middle of a whiskey bottle (a round bottle works best), leaving about an inch of twine hanging down from the knot. Light this little end piece, allow the twine to catch fire all the way around the bottle, then shove the bottle into a bucket of cold water. The bottle will break clean where the string was tied, and the bottom half can be used for a drinking glass. Smooth the rough-cut rim with a piece of sandstone.

FIRE STARTER

When you're out hunting or hiking in the deep woods, waterproofed matches and a fire starter can be a help in the rain. Take a bunch of blue-tipped strike-anywhere matches, coat them in melted wax to make them watertight, and bring 000 steel wool as a waterproof fire starter. Put the steel wool under some twigs, touch your match to it, then blow. The steel wool will glow red-hot and start your fire even if the wool itself is wet.

WATER FROM A VINE

Clear, tasty water can be bled from a muscadine vine by cutting into it and letting it drain into a container. To use the vine as a reliable source of water in the future, be sure not to kill it. Arrange a hanging vine in a "U" shape, and cut partway into the bottom of the "U." Water will drip out steadily, and the vine will stay healthy. Recut as necessary. Some vines are said to run like a tap lightly turned on.

WHEN YOU CAN'T FIND YOUR WAY HOME

"If you are ever lost in the woods, remember that the pileated wood-pecker digs his home facing east, a flying squirrel's hole is usually facing east, a spider's web is usually facing south, the rings on a cut-down tree most often show a greater growth on north and northeast sides, and the tops of evergreen trees usually bend to the east." (Thomas B., age thirteen)

REMEDIES

Back in the early days people had to guzzle whiskey, douse themselves with turpentine, and boil tree roots to relieve themselves of common ailments. All across America different communities swore by many of the same remedies. Some of them are clearly ridiculous, but a lot actually contain active ingredients similar to those in modern medicines. For example, garlic, also known as the poor man's antibiotic, actually kills bacteria. So next time someone tells you to rub a potato on a steam burn or that beets cure cancer, don't be so quick to call it hooey.

Ridiculous, right?
Take this test to see how much you really know . . .

1. To cure an earache, warm a spoonful of urine and put a few drops in your ear.   True ❏   False ❏
2. It's better to treat a black eye with a hunk of raw refrigerated meat than with a popsicle.   True ❏   False ❏
3. Rinsing your hair with vinegar helps treat a bad case of dandruff.   True ❏   False ❏
4. You can remove a sty by running the tip of a black cat's tail over your eye.   True ❏   False ❏

5. If you tie a rhubarb root around your neck with a string, you won't get stomachaches. True ❏   False ❏

6. Ingesting a fistful of charcoal should mop up a case of the runs. True ❏   False ❏

7. Strawberries and cherries relieve gout. True ❏   False ❏

8. Relieve nocturnal heartburn by stuffing telephone books under the head end of your mattress. True ❏   False ❏

9. Eat peas to relieve symptoms of female menopause.
   True ❏   False ❏

10. Staunch heavy blood flow from a wound with wet tea bags.
    True ❏   False ❏

11. To kill the infection in a wound pour turpentine on it.
    True ❏   False ❏

12. Tie a red onion around your bedpost, and you won't catch cold. True ❏   False ❏

13. Lie down flat on your back, and put a dime over your heart to stop a nosebleed. True ❏   False ❏

14. If you cut yourself badly, have a dog lick your wound to heal it. True ❏   False ❏

15. Put axle grease on a burn to help it heal.
    True ❏   False ❏

16. Eating kudzu root will help cure your cravings for booze.
    True ❏   False ❏

17. Put a spider web on a wound to stop it from bleeding.
    True ❏   False ❏

18. Make willow tea to cure a headache or break a fever.
    True ❏   False ❏

19. Drink whiskey to counteract snake venom.
    True ❏   False ❏

20. Letting moonlight bathe your face while you're sleeping will cause you to go crazy. True ❏   False ❏

ANSWERS:

1. **False.** Warm piss won't cure an earache, but if your ear is blocked, vinegar or vegetable oil can help break down the wax.

2. **False.** Lots of folk remedies prescribe raw meat for bumps and bruises, but there is nothing in the meat that actually helps healing; it's the coolness of the meat people are after. In reality something frozen, even a popsicle, will slow the internal bleeding more effectively.

3. **True.** Dandruff occurs because of an overly alkaline condition in the scalp. Rinsing the hair with vinegar should help. Crushing up an aspirin (salicylic acid) and putting it in your shampoo bottle can also help.

4. **False.** This sort of thing is called *sympathetic* or *contagious* magic, which means trying to transfer illness to an animal, plant, another object, or, even, maliciously, to someone else. Another contagious magic remedy to eliminate warts is to rub them with a stolen dishrag, and the rag owner will get the warts.

5. **False.** Sure, and if you let a black chicken fly over you after the sun goes down, it'll bring out the chicken pox.

6. **True.** Charcoal (the pure stuff, not what you put on the BBQ) absorbs toxins, including diarrhea-causing ones. In hospitals charcoal is used to treat drug overdose patients. The downside is that it also absorbs essential vitamins and minerals.

7. **True.** Gout is caused by a buildup of uric acid, particularly in the joints. Strawberries and cherries contain an enzyme that neutralizes uric acid.

8. **True.** Gravity keeps the digestive acids where they belong: in the stomach.

9. **True.** Peas have a lot of natural estrogen in them, which the female body needs when going through menopause.

10. **True.** Wet tea bags contain tannin, which helps blood to coagulate.

11. **True.** Turpentine does kill infection. And while that's fine on the skin, it's probably not a good idea to take it internally. It's a very concentrated substance and can be poisonous if there is too much in the bloodstream . . .

12. **False.** Red onions smell bad to us, not to bacteria.

13. **True.** This will actually work, but not because of the dime. It's because you're lying down.

14. **True.** Licking your own wound, or having a dog lick it is actually a good thing, if you don't have access to proper medication. Most mouths (dog and human) do not carry enough germs to be harmful to the person they are licking, and saliva has long been known to speed healing. Any oral surgeon will tell you that saliva is antibacterial and part of the immune system. Saliva contains proteins and enzymes with digestive and antibiotic functions.

15. **False.** Never put grease on a burn. It will only make it worse.

16. **True.** Kudzu, that wild vine that grows all over the American South, has recently been proven by the Center for Biochemical and Biophysical Sciences and Medicine at Harvard University to suppress alcohol cravings in biochemically addicted rodents. The active ingredient is an isoflavonone called diadzin.

17. **False.** While spiders (especially venomous ones) have plenty of medicinal value, their delicate webs are not of much use.

18. **True.** Willow bark and leaves are high in salicylic acid, which is aspirin.

19. **False.** For venomous snakebite victims, old-time doctors prescribed a quart of whiskey to be drunk within twenty-four hours. Bad idea. While the AMS has reported findings that alcohol is helpful in fighting the early stages of the common cold, it dilates blood vessels and speeds up circulation, actually intensifying the effect of the venom.

20. **False.** Though emergency rooms HAVE long been known to be busier during full moons. And, by the way, if someone calls you a "mooncalf," it's not a compliment . . . it's Shakespeare-ese for "retard."

Turpentine

"Turpentine stole a lot of money from the doctors in those days, as I'm sure it could today if the AMA didn't poo-poo its use."
—RUSTY O., turpentine user

Turpentine is distilled pine pitch from the slash and longleaf pines. Oil of turpentine was widely used in the old days as a stimulant, diuretic, anti-spasmodic, wound disinfectant, and astringent. Some still claim a spoonful a day cures arthritis and destroys intestinal parasites. Of course, before you start drinking it, consider its current most popular use: paint thinner.

ENDNOTE

The Tale of the Ingenious Wolf

Farmer Giles was sitting out by a lake when he saw a wolf carefully pick a piece of sheep wool off a barbed wire fence. Holding the wool in his mouth the wolf went down to the water. Very slowly the wolf started backing in until he was completely submerged except for the wool. Then he let the wool go and swam away. Curious, the farmer fished the wool out of the water and found that it was full of fleas.

FURTHER READING

NONFICTION

America Bizarro by Nelson Taylor

The Anarchist Cookbook by William Powell

The Book of Stock Car Wisdom edited by Criswell Freeman

A Childhood: Biography of a Place by Harry Crews

Dolly by Dolly Parton

Ecology of a Cracker Childhood by Janisse Ray

Fast as White Lightning by Kim Chapin

The Foxfire Book edited by Elliott Wiggington

Honey, Mud, Maggots, and other Medical Marvels by Robert
 Root-Bernstein

The Kandy-Kolored Tangerine-Flake Streamline, Baby by Tom Wolfe

*Manifold Destiny: The One the Only Guide to Cooking on Your Car
 Engine* by Chris Maynard

Polish Your Furniture with Pantyhose by Joey Green

Redneck Heaven by Bethany Bultman

The Straight Dope books by Cecil Adams

Wheel Estate: The Rise and Decline of Mobile Homes by Alan Wallis

FICTION

The Adventures of Huckleberry Finn by Mark Twain

A Feast of Snakes by Harry Crews

Boy with Loaded Gun by Lewis Nordan
Sometimes a Great Notion by Ken Kesey
Trailerpark by Russell Banks

WEB SITES
MissouriTrailerTrash.com
MidwestMonsters.com
Snopes.com

PLACES TO VISIT
The Art Car Museum, Houston, TX
Smokey Mountain Car Museum, Pigeon Forge, TN
Paradise Gardens, Summerville, GA
The Orange Show, Houston TX
Grandma Prisbey's Bottle Village, Simi Valley, CA
Salvation Mountain, Niland, CA
SPAM Museum, Austin, MN